Bulletin

EAST MIDWOOD JEWISH CENTER

SHAARE TORAH
THEY SHALL BUILD ME A SANCTUARY • AND I SHALL DWELL AMONG THEM

June, 1981   Sivan, 5741

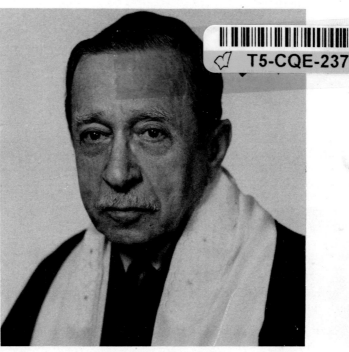

In Memoriam
Rabbi Harry Halpern
1899-1981

"The Memory of the Righteous
Shall be for A Blessing"

Rabbi Harry Halpern

Following Rabbi Halpern's funeral on Friday, June 12th, 1981, we seriously considered postponing the Annual Installation of Officers and Trustees originally scheduled to take place on Saturday, June 13th.

We decided that our beloved Rabbi Halpern would wish to make sure that the wheels of administration maintain their continuity, and so we held our Installation as planned.

My wife Helen, my two daughters and I have been affiliated with the East Midwood Jewish Center for a quarter of a century, and our association with Rabbi Halpern has touched every phase of our lives. He officiated at the wedding of our daughter, he graced our simchas, and comforted us in illness and in sorrow.

I know I speak for all our members who from time to time have experienced the loving tender care of Rabbi Halpern on many similar happenings.

As Rabbi he spent many hours in his Center office giving advice to families in trouble, and making appropriate referrals to other agencies where prolonged treatment was indicated.

I shall always remember his interest in, and devotion to, the children attending the Rabbi Harry Halpern Day School. He spent many hours daily in his school office. It was not unusual for him to sit next to a new student, who was somewhat fearful of the new experience, to hug and hold a youngster affectionately, wiping a tear, or wiping a nose or tying a shoelace. He knew the name of every child, engaging them in pleasant conversation, giving them the feeling of belonging, and of being welcome.

The plans for the funeral services of Rabbi Halpern that took place in our synagogue on Friday were prepared by Rabbi Halpern long before and were followed exactly as he had set forth. His request for the blowing of the Shofar may have many meanings. The obituary notices from organizations and individuals described Rabbi Halpern as a scholar, a brilliant speaker, teacher, and a dynamic community leader. He was also described as a man of great wit, possessing a keen sense of humor, and inspiration to all who were fortunate to be in his company, a supporter of Israel and Zionism, a pioneering religious educator, aand a passionate advocate of human rights.

We are all diminished by his leaving us. We will never forget the hours we spent together in happy fellowship. May we forever cherish the memory of Rabbi Halpern's loyalty and love for us individually and collectively, and for all mankind.

On behalf of the Officers, Trustees, members and the entire staff, I extend our heartfelt sympathies and condolences to his wife Jean and daughter Debbie and their families.

Milton Krasne
President

𝕽𝖆𝖇𝖇𝖎 𝕳𝖆𝖗𝖗𝖞 𝕳𝖆𝖑𝖕𝖊𝖗𝖓

All of us at the East Midwood Jewish Center deeply mourn the passing of our esteemed and beloved Rabbi Emeritus Harry Halpern. For almost a half century, he served with extraordinary zeal and ability as our spiritual leader, teacher, guide, and friend. His eloquence, erudition, and fervor inspired us and uplifted us; his enthusiasm increased our joys; and his compassion minimized our sadness. His leadership made this synagogue a paragon of excellence throughout the country. His love of children and Jewish education led to the establishment of the Rabbi Harry Halpern Day School of the East Midwood Jewish Center which has for a quarter of a century been in the vanguard of the day school movement in America. His abilities were widely recognized from one shore to the other and made him an influential spokesman in behalf of the American Jewish community, as well as a passionate supporter of Israel.

The officers, trustees, members, and professional staff extend our heartfelt condolences to his wife Jean, his daughter, Debbie Silverman and his granddaughter, Meredith, and all the other members of his family. Even as we mourn his death, we celebrate his exemplary life and are grateful for the role he played in our lives. May his soul be forever bound up in the bond of everlasting life; and may his soul endure in our midst as a source of eternal benediction.

Dr. Alvin Kass, Rabbi

Reprinted from *The New York Times*

Dr. Alvin Kass · Rabbi
President · Milton Krasne
Executive Director · Bernard Panzer
Educational Director · Dr. Aryeh Rohn

Cantor · Joseph Eidelson
Assoc. Cantor · Rev. Joseph Mayer
Editor · Herman Brenner

Assoc. Editors: Rabbi Kass, Dr. Aryeh Rohn, Dr. Hyman B. Ritchin Contributing Editors: Belle Miller, Hazel Plan. The Bulletin of the East Midwood Jewish Center, 1625 Ocean Avenue, Brooklyn, New York, 11230 is published bi-weekly, from the beginning of Center activities in the Fall to the end of Center activities in the Spring except weeks of religious holidays. Subscription price is $4.00 per annum. Second class postage paid at Brooklyn, New York. Pub. Number 076100. Affiliated with the United Synagogue of America.

RABBI HALPERN

Twenty-two years of work with a man provide sufficient evidence of the many images he portrays. There was the demonstration of what may be called the "touch of Greatness". There was the evidence of strength and weakness, of love, anger, wisdom, frustration, and all human qualities. Here was a leader, a guiding spirit, and a teacher. Let all the following personal experiences speak for themselves.

My first week of work in East Midwood, September 1956, an angry voice on the phone exclaimed, "Dear Sir, it is about time that the Committee on UnAmerican Activities of the Congress ceased to exist. My name was proudly displayed in the New York Times supporting this opinion. I shall not come to Washington, neither am I interested in meeting you here." These were the words spoken by Rabbi Halpern to the Counsel of the Committee on UnAmerican Activities of the Congress. This is one of the many expressions of the courage of the man.

The day after Yom Kippur 1973, the Synagogue was crowded, and many people had to stand in the rear. Rabbi Halpern's words analyzed the situation is Israel and neighboring countries. Our hearts were filled with worry and concern for our brethren in israel. Then followed words of encouragement which lifted our spirits. We all felt that we had to do something special for our brethren in Israel. "If I have ever been able to teach you something in these 40 years of my service to you, and if I have ever had some influence on you, then open your hearts, and give tonight." And the hearts felt warm and good, and the donations came in great numbers to support the State of Israel, in its hour of crisis and danger.

This was the master of oratory speaking to his congregation. This was the voice of the Jewish conscience.

However, the private man appeared to us in the way he dealt with children and parents. When Rabbi Halpern entered the School Building in the morning his first destination was the Kindergarten. There was an outpouring of love and affection which had to be seen to be believed. Every child waited anxiously for Rabbi Halpern to visit.

Many a parent drew the wrath of Rabbi Halpern when arriving late to pick up children, who waited impatiently. How often did I hear the words, "A good mother does not let a little child wait. You must be on time."

Who has ever seen a prominent Rabbi waiting on children in the lunchroom. This was one rabbi who understood children of all ages. He was ready to substitute for absent teachers, and when I myself had to leave he would say, "Geht gezunt and kum gezunt". (Go in good health, and come back in good health), and I knew I could be absent and everything would be taken care of.

Hundreds of troubled teenagers, young adults, and mature people came to his office, to ask for advice, for guidance and encouragement. I am witness to the thousands of hours spent on these tasks, and I was witness to the hopeful faces which appeared from his office after a talk with him.

This was the man with whom I had the privilege of working for twenty years.

May his memory be blessed.

Dr. Aryeh Rohn
Educational Director

FROM WHERE I STAND

"The Rabbi's Personal Column"

What is faith? As the word is generally understood, it means acknowledgement of the existence of a Supreme Being and the reality of a divine order in the world. It means a religious system or a religious group to which one belongs. But faith means more than this. It conveys the idea of the certainty of goodness. To have faith in some person or thing means to be sure of his or its goodness. It means to accept as true that which cannot be demonstrated by rational proof or tangible evidence.

What is faith? It is the ability to say in the hour of sorrow that life is good, and that pain and bereavement are a natural part thereof. It is a rendering of thanks for the blessings we have enjoyed rather than a vain yearning after those we might have had.

What is faith? It is the recognition that the quality of a life is infinitely more important than its number of years. It is the memory of precious moments stored up in the heart, unforgettable experiences which punctuate the ordinary prose of life and give it meaning.

What is faith? It is the determination to make ideals live long after the one who professed them is no longer in existence. It is the ability to find solace in the association of the afflicted.

What is faith? It is the ability to feel the touch of a hand made cold by death, to hear across the great barrier the gentle, soothing voice of those we loved. It is the ability to face the trials of life with courage and to confront its problems with undimmed eye.

This is the meaning of faith.

Rabbi Halpern's dedication to humanity is reflected in his deeds and writings. He was one of the first to recognize the potential value of the congregational bulletin as an educational tool. For over forty years his column, the nationally respected "From Where I Stand" gave voice to his beliefs.

Rabbi Halpern's book, "FROM WHERE I STAND" printed in 1974 by the Ktav Publishing House Inc., New York, is a compilation of one hundred and sixty of the best of these intellectually and spiritually inspiring columns. It is available in the East Midwood Book Store.

FROM WHERE I STAND

"The Rabbi's Personal Column"

Israel — This is my people. A people which has suffered and sacrificed, and fought and bled, and lived and died for the sake of an ideal.

This is my people, a peculiar, complex, mysterious people. It celebrates joyous festivals and ends them with memorial prayers for the dead. Its happy marriage rite is concluded by the reminder of an ancient tragedy, the destruction of its glorious sanctuary.

This is my people — individuals who have been accused of dishonest business dealings and who are commanded not to defraud another in the slightest way; a people whose constant greeting is "Peace" and yet has been accused of being bloodthirsty and militaristic.

This is my people — human beings who have healed the wounds and afflictions of their enemies but whose own members are persecuted and tortured by others.

This is my people — men and women, with the brand of tyranny upon their arms, hunted, persecuted, and exiled, yet finding few friends among the nations of the world — a people which more than all others is the symbol and victim of the struggles of great powers for world domination. This is a people which talks of milk and honey while all others talk of oil.

This is my people — a collection of diverse human beings, pitifully small numerically and yet able to withstand the onslaught of vastly superior numbers.

This is my people — storekeepers, tradesmen, and students who overnight become farmers and fighters, who transform arid deserts into flourishing cities, and wastelands into gardens.

This is my people — persons who constantly long for peace and are never permitted for a long time to enjoy it.

This is my people — which loses when it wins and wins when it loses, which must surrender hard-won gains against its will, but on the other hand is able to win the esteem and respect of those who appreciate determination and valor.

This is my people, a people which can look death in the eye, unafraid, and march to certain death, singing, "Ani Ma-amin" ("I believe"), expressing the unshakeable conviction that peace and brotherly love will eventually prevail in the world.

Yes, this is my people; and with all its suffering, I can affirm that I would rather be a humble citizen in Meah Shearim than a commissar in Leningrad.

FROM WHERE I STAND

"The Rabbi's Personal Column"

Memory is a divine gift bestowed on man in order to save his life from becoming a meaningless procession of unconnected events. It is the faculty which enables us to make of the past a present reality and to see time as an endless flow of the life process. The sights which we behold, the sounds we hear, the joy we experience — all of these would be merely pictures, projected on life's screen, to be quickly erased, were it not for the power of memory.

Fortunately, we, as human beings, have been given the ability to recall the sun's brilliant rays after it has set, to hear the melody which survives the instrument which has produced it, to feel the glow of a happiness which has departed. It is memory which acts as manna from heaven to nourish the famished spirit, traveling in the wastelands of life.

What is the history of a people but its common memories etched deeply in the mind? The Jews, who were probably the first people on earth with a sense of history, understood the need for preserving memories. In all his festivals, the Jew was reminded of his past. He recognized that the present was a continuation of the past and a preparation for the future. The present tense of the Hebrew verb is as much an adjective as a verb.

It must be admitted, however, that memory does not always bring joy. It may serve to illumine once more some dark corner of the past which it were best to leave in obscurity. Nevertheless, even this is important for a muature person because it teaches us humility in the presence of life, it makes us aware of the price which living demands and of man's precarious situation.

No event of any significance happens to us without leaving some trace behind. We try hard to remember the joys and would like to obliterate the sorrows, but both survive in the mind. For some, the tracings are clear; while with others the impressions are dim. The letters of the Hebrew word meaning "to forget," if rearranged slightly, spell the word meaning "to darken." Forgetfulness means plunging a past experience into darkness, while memory means to see it in a clear light. To be able to say, "I remember," marks one as a human being.

RABBI HARRY HALPERN

Rabbi Halpern, the spiritual leader of the East Midwood Jewish Center in Brooklyn for 49 years until his retirement in 1977, was also adjunct professor of pastoral psychiatry at the Jewish Theological Seminary of America at the time of his death.

Rabbi Halpern had been president of the New York Board of Rabbis and the Rabbinical Assembly of America as well as member of the executive committees of both the Brooklyn Red Cross and the Brooklyn Cancer Society.

A former member of the Kings County Advisory Council of the New York State Commission Against Discrimination, Rabbi Halpern served on the Human Rights Commission from 1967 to 1978. He was also a member of the executive committee of the New York Division of the National Conference of Christians and Jews.

Rabbi Halpern had also been chairman of the Rabbinic Cabinet of the Jewish Theological Seminary, where he first was a visiting professor of homiletics, before becoming adjunct professor of pastoral psychiatry. He was also past chairman of the board of the Yeshiva of Flatbush.

As chairman of the Social Action Commission of Conservative Judaism, Rabbi Halpern strongly opposed proposals for Federal aid to private and religious schools.

The rabbi was born in New York City. He received a bachelor's degree from the College of the City of New York in 1919 and a master's degree from Columbia University in 1925. He studied at the Rabbi Isaac Elchanan Theological Seminary and was ordained in 1929 by the Jewish Theological Seminary of America. In 1951, Rabbi Halpern received a Doctor of Hebrew Literature degree from the Jewish Theological Seminary. In addition, he received bachelor and doctoral degrees from Brooklyn Law School.

Rabbi Halpern is survived by his wife, Jean; a daughter, Deborah Silverman, by his previous marriage to the late Mollie Singer Halpern; two step-daughters, Myra and Caren Rosenhaus; two brothers, Rabbi Peretz Halpern of Marblehead, Mass., and Isadore Halpern of Brooklyn, and a grandchild.

New York Times
June 12, 1981

"Let Your Reverence For Your Teacher
Be Equal To Your Reverence for God"

Bulletin—East Midwood J.C.
1625 Ocean Avenue
Brooklyn, N.Y. 11230

2nd Class Postage Paid
Brooklyn, N.Y.

Mrs. Mindu Waltman
1362 - 45th St.
Brooklyn 19, N. Y.   11219

TIME VALUE

To
Mindu,
a teacher,
11:58 to 12
a thoughtful, gentle
human being, accept-
able by both children
and parents, but above
all a warm person who
has won the hearts of all
who know her, with best
wishes. Harry Halpern
June 1974
3° Feb 31 Nt

FROM WHERE I STAND

FROM WHERE I STAND

HARRY HALPERN

KTAV PUBLISHING HOUSE, INC.
NEW YORK

SBN 87068-263-6

LIBRARY OF CONGRESS CATALOG CARD NUMBER; 74-6397
MANUFACTURED IN THE UNITED STATES OF AMERICA

CONTENTS

INTRODUCTION   IX

A MAN AND HIS NEIGHBORS   1

HOLIDAYS AND OBSERVANCES   23

RELIGION   65

THE PERSONAL LIFE   101

TIME   175

To Mollie, in remembrance
and to
Jean, Debbie, Alan, Myra and Caren,
in love

INTRODUCTION

The congregational bulletin is a unique innovation in American Jewish life which has become an established institution in the United States. For many of our people it is not only a reminder of the congregational calendar, but an important source, sometimes the only source, of Jewish information.

This development has taken place because many rabbis are now writing regular columns or articles in their bulletins about Jewish and other matters. In this way, the American rabbi reaches more of his congregants than by his preaching, since only a small percentage of them attends religious services with any great degree of regularity.

Rabbi Harry Halpern was one of the first men in this country to understand the potential value which the congregational bulletin has as an educational tool. More than four decades ago, he began writing a regular column for his weekly congregational publication. Since then, these articles have appeared week after week.

Readers of these articles, a collection of which is now presented in this book, will readily recognize why they have been so well received. Many of them show originality of thought and deep perception. The author is alert to the minutest details of life around him. He writes about the ephemeral and the eternal. In each article one feels the directness and the outspoken approach. The author is forthright and expresses his opinions without equivocation. His intense Jewish commitment is obvious.

Rabbi Harry Halpern is one of those rare men who has established a reputation in two areas. He has long been known as a gifted preacher of rare imagination and singular talent. Over the years, he has also gained fame for the weekly column which he has been writing for his congregational bulletin. The greatest tribute to his efforts is the fact that so many of his colleagues are among his most devoted readers.

This volume will afford the readers of the author's articles a selection of them in more permanent form. It will also offer others the opportunity to become acquainted with the work of an eloquent and articulate spokesman of American Jewry.

Peretz Halpern

A MAN and HIS NEIGHBORS

A little boy walking out of his home slammed the door. This is not unusual for youngsters of his age, although it can be annoying to grown-ups. To learn how to close doors gently is part of being well-mannered.

The closing of the door made me think of situations which it symbolizes. Doors are used to divide rooms from one another; they reveal the various activities of home life. They shut us off from the world outside and give us privacy. But the ability to close a door properly has even wider implications.

All of us, at some time in our lives, are involved in errors or grief. There are many, alas too many, people, who continue to live under the shadow of sadness They fail to recognize that we must have the ability to shut the door on the unpleasantness of the past. If the door is left open, we can be pursued by what is behind it. To be able to say of something undesirable, "It is over," is an important step in attaining maturity.

There are all kinds of doors. Some have a glass panel so that while we may be shut off from what is on the other side, we are still able to see what is there. Perhaps in time it may not be altogether harmful to look back at an unpleasant past, provided we have first shut the door. But there is also a diabolical contraption called the revolving door. You step into it, and if you don't get out at the proper moment, you find yourself back where you started. To make progress in life means to know when to leave the door; otherwise one will be constantly moving without effecting any change of place.

There are many other fascinating ideas that are symbolized by doors. But it should be pointed out that they are not merely the means of shutting off the past and the old but also opportunities for stepping into the future and the new. A door is a transition and a connecting link.

No doubt it is the recognition of the important transition from the world outside to the sanctuary of home and vice versa, that is responsible for the affixing of a mezuzah on the door post of Jewish homes. Besides the reason for it which is mentioned in the Bible, it also says to all who see it, "On the other side of this door there is love, unselfishness, cooperation, and family life." And, looking out, it says, "On the other side of this door is the wide world where you must practice the things you have learned in this home."

3

Somewhere in or near Memphis, Tennessee, there is a man, probably a young one, who is proud of his marksmanship. With one shot he ended the life of one of the truly great leaders of our age and plunged the majority of the American people into grief. A nation stands aghast at the useless, brutal, racist murder of the lamented Martin Luther King.

Why did Dr. King lose his life? Was he trying to instigate riots? Did he advocate violent means of achieving his objectives? Did he urge Negroes to ask for anything to which they were not entitled? To all these questions, the answer is in the negative. In spite of verbal attacks by the leaders of militant groups and in the face of provocation by irresponsible individuals, challenged by the recognition of frustrated hopes and broken promises, deeply touched by the plight of his people, Martin Luther King adhered, to the last moment of his life, to the doctrine of non-violence. A little over a week ago, at the annual convention of the Rabbinical Assembly of America, we heard him eloquently reaffirm his conviction that whatever the Negro may hope to achieve should be and would be done only through non-violence. His was a truly religious approach to the social problems of our time. He struggled for equal rights for black people, he opposed the bloodshed of Vietnam, and he openly espoused the cause of Israel.

In introducing him to a United Synagogue convention in 1963, I called attention to a Midrashic statement. In it, the rabbis say of the burning bush Moses saw, that it was burning with a heavenly fire, a fire which burns but does not consume. This was the zeal that animated Dr. King. It burned with intensity, but consumed no one. The Rabbis say also that earthly fire is red but the fire of the burning bush was black. There, where God revealed Himself to Moses, was black fire. In contemporary terms we might say that we see God revealed in the struggle of our Negro brethren for that freedom which is the right of every human being.

There are two Hebrew words which are spelled with the same letters, and the only difference between them is merely a matter of punctuation. One is the word *shachor,* which means ."black," and the other is the word *shachar,* which means "dawn." There can be no greater or more appropriate tribute to the memory of a martyred leader than to make the struggle of the *shachor,* the Negro, the *shachar,* the dawn of a new day for all Americans no matter what their race or creed, a day in which inequity will be abolished and men will take their place as equals before their fellowmen. Until and unless that happens, I, as an American, must hang my head and weep for the stain on the shield of my country.

The word "communication" is being used with increasing frequency in our daily speech. In its usual sense it denotes a verbal or written message or an exchange of information. But it can also be used in another way. It can mean making oneself understood to another human being, achieving rapport with one's fellowman, breaking down the walls that separate one human being from another.

With all the progress that has been made in the study and understanding of the wellsprings of human behavior, of the emotions and thinking processes of men, of what it is that makes people what they are, there still remain unexplored areas that defy human probing. We must admit that man is still an enigma, and that we must therefore be circumspect in judging others whose innermost thoughts must remain inaccessible to us.

The human mind is a wide expanse over which weird notions, noble thoughts, selfish desires, depressing reflections, and soothing insights travel during our waking and sleeping hours. Within us is a battlefield on which conflicting emotions struggle for victory. If we know this from our own experience, why can't we, then, try to understand that others pass through the same trials?

Despite all obstacles, we must try to communicate with others. We must do our best to make our fellowmen realize that we are trying to understand them. This does not demand many words or eloquent speech. It can be done often by a simple gesture.

In the eighth century before the Christian era, King Hezekiah built a conduit which brought water from a spring to the Pool of Siloam. The record of the tunneling is recorded on a wall of the tunnel. It describes how two groups of workmen bored from opposite sides. "While yet there were three cubits to be bored through, there was heard the voice of one calling unto another. And on the day of the boring through, the stonecutters struck, each to meet his fellow."

With sympathy and a sincere desire to meet our fellowmen, we might start working from our side while others work from theirs. If our spiritual engineering is accurate, we shall hear each other's voices and meet, thus making it possible for the waters of understanding to flow from man to his neighbor.

In the course of a conversation with a man recently, the phrase "telling it as it is" was used frequently. It is an expression which has become part of the daily vocabulary of most people. But I am trying to understand exactly what the words mean.

In a general way, I suppose, they mean, to be realistic, to see things clearly, to rid oneself of illusions. This attitude is based upon the assumption that what we see and hear and experience constitute the total picture of life. There is nothing beyond what is here and now, and if one perceives anything else, he is either a weak-minded individual who cannot face reality or a starry-eyed visionary.

This is perhaps one of the major faults of our time, that we see only isolated facts and experiences without realizing that they are meaningless unless we already have a framework for them. The facts alone are not merely insignificant, but they will be seen differently by different people. To put it briefly, the most important element in the life of an individual is his view of the world and of life. To see something "as it is" means not only to behold with the eyes but also to bring a certain feeling to it. This may be illustrated by our attitude to people.

Do we really see others as they are? What does "as they are" mean? Does one objectively collect data about a person in his mind, and then, compiling certain character traits, decide that one loves another human being? Is it not closer to the truth to say that first we love another person and then we find those characteristics and traits which justify our emotional reaction to him or her? We assume that a pessimist is one who has had a difficult life, who has suffered misfortune, and who has not succeeded. We will find, I think, that one has a pessimistic attitude toward life to begin with and then finds certain experiences that will, in his

6

opinion, bolster his unhappy reaction toward life. The rain that nurtures the grass and flowers is welcomed by those who are interested in verdure, but is the bane of those who see in it the creator of mud puddles and a source of inconvenience. If one were to "tell it as it is" about love and bitterness and rain, the reality would depend upon the attitude of the seer or the hearer. It is very important to remember this at a time when there is so much hostility in the world which men try to explain by "telling it as it is," but which is, in truth, the result of selecting facts on the basis of a previously adopted emotional attitude.

Most people are so busily engaged in daily pursuits that they fail to look for the larger scheme into which to fit them. In every situation there is a mystical, poetic, incomprehensible element which must be considered. Love and hatred, enthusiasm and apathy are the results of what can be called our religious attitude. Despite our scientific spirit and devotion to experimentation, we must recognize that there are first principles, which like mathematical axioms must precede all deductions. Religion of any kind asks the fundamental question, "What is your attitude toward life?" Every mature human being must answer that question before he can go about the business of living. Despite all assertions to the contrary, we must admit that what things really are will depend to a great extent on what we and our attitudes are.

A child is being punished for some offense which is an infringement of the rules by which conduct in the class is governed. One asks the culprit the reason for the misbehavior. Invariably the answer given points to the misunderstanding or downright meanness of the teacher, the conduct of a classmate, or some circumstance beyond the child's control. There is hardly ever an occasion when the child says, "I was wrong."

We grow up and we carry this attitude with us into our mature lives. If we do anything which is socially unacceptable or unworthy in our own sight, we lay the blame at the door of external conditions or on the shoulders of others. Does this mean that we are lying? Not at all. We, like the child, are sincerely convinced ourselves that we are not to blame.

This obtuseness to personal responsibility stems from the fact that we feel our superiority to others. We lack the humility to confess that we are mortals who often err. To admit that we may be wrong is deemed an admission of inadequacy. The lazy person who is asked to bestir himself and go about the business of life says, in the words of Proverbs, "There is a lion outside." We hug to our hearts the image of perfection we see in ourselves. What makes this attitude most harmful is not so much that we conceal it from others but that we ourselves are not conscious of it.

Everything substantial casts a shadow, and if we have no shadow we have no substance. Every life has its dark side, and it is a healthy person who is conscious of it. From this point of view, confession is not only "good for the soul," as a popular phrase has it, it is healthful for man's total life.

I am certain that the Psalmist felt great relief when he cried out to his Maker, "Thou hast set our iniquities before Thee, our secret sins in the light of Thy countenance." With this attitude we may learn to be more concerned with saving our own souls than in constantly endeavoring to rescue the souls of others.

I remember the story of a man who had sailed across the ocean and was narrating a personal experience. He was walking on the deck one day and he heard a cry, "Man overboard!" "I took one look," he said, "and discovered that I was in the water."

When we discuss the sins of others, and plan to save them, it is well that we should first take a good look. We ourselves may be in the water.

WHAT IS LOVE?

What is love?

The dictionary defines love as a feeling of strong personal attachment based upon that which delights or commands admiration. But the emotion involves much more.

What is love?

It is joy in something or someone for its or his own sake. To do something "for love" means to expect no other reward than the love itself.

What is love?

It means the breaking of bonds which keep us within ourselves and the going forth of one's spirit into the life of another, without losing one's identity in the other.

What is love?

It is that which makes us more truly ourselves than we were before, that which elicits the noblest within us.

What is love?

It is the highest form of active unselfishness.

What is love?

It is the ability to see another being realistically, to understand him completely, and to forgive him religiously.

What is love?

It is the capacity to adore another person without indulging in idolatry.

What is love?

It is the strength to sacrifice for another even if there be no appreciation of the sacrifice.

What is love?

It is a human being's total commitment to another "with all his heart, with all his soul, and with all his might."

What is love?

It is the feeling that the world says "Amen" to our choice, and that God's finger is tapping us on the shoulder.

What is love?

It is the power to see even sorrow as the search for a lost joy.

What is love?

It means the ability to confer immortality on a memory.

This is the meaning of love.

Deeply imbedded in the heart of a great many people is a perversity which renders them incapable of gratitude. For some reason incomprehensible to me, human beings fail to render thanks for what is done in their behalf. Since I have encountered this tendency quite often, I have been led to speculate upon its sources.

It may be that those for whom something is done are convinced that it was owed them. They reason that what we do in their behalf is no more than an obligation that we are bound to discharge. Or it may be that in acknowledging their indebtedness, some people feel that they are confessing to a certain dependence upon others.

Whatever we do to help our fellowmen should not be done in the hope of getting rewarded for our efforts in the form of honors, financial gain, or by other types of recognition. But, on the other hand, we have a right to expect that those for whom we exert ourselves should, at least, render gratitude for what is done. If this is not forthcoming, one feels deeply hurt.

In one of his plays, Shakespeare puts these words into the mouth of one of his characters:

> Blow, blow, thou winter wind;
> Thou art not so unkind
> As man's ingratitude.

Perhaps it is this inability to give thanks that is the greatest obstacle to true prayer. It can be asserted, I think, that the major portion of our prayer book consists of an expression of thanks for what we have received at the hands of God and not of requests for blessings or favors. The Talmud says that in the era in the future when the entire sacrificial system will disappear, one form of sacrifice will remain, viz., the offering of thanksgiving.

To accept the favors which are bestowed upon us without any acknowledgment on our part is to be guilty of a sin against God and our fellowmen. But, I suppose, one has no right to expect gratitude. One should be grateful for the fact that the people from whom he should expect gratitude do not add hostility to their ingratitude. There's always something for which to be thankful.

10

A group of distinguished scientists has just begun a campaign to raise funds for educating the public to the dangers of the atomic bomb. Since the information will be furnished by those whose research made the bomb possible, it will carry great weight. This latest effort comes on the heels of many similar ones, all concerned with making clear that the only alternative to world peace is complete annihilation of our civilization.

In numerous books and articles we have been told that the division of the uranium atom has created the greatest problem of our time. Yet, it seems to me that there is one which is even more fundamental, and which existed even before the Manhattan Project was completed. The national rivalries, the quest for foreign markets, the conflict of divergent economic theories—all these were in existence before the deadly missile fell on Hiroshima. To me it seems that the underlying problem is that of the righteous use of power.

In every department of human life, the weal or woe of men is determined by the manner in which those who possess power, exercise it. In the sphere of politics, untold misery has come to millions because of the abuse of power by those in control. It matters not what form the coercion or oppression may take, or whether the unrighteous mandate of the ruler is enforceable through the might of a vast army or by the streamlined method of the atomic bomb. The important consideration is that if those who possess power use it for selfish ends, then there cannot be a peaceful world.

The economic scene presents us with the same difficulties. Frequently, capital uses the power of its money, and labor utilizes its mass pressure, in reckless disregard of the welfare of the general public, which is caught between the upper and lower millstones of our economic system. If only those who wield power could be made to realize the tremendous good which they could confer by its beneficent use!

It is one of the tragedies of political life that power is so frequently misused. Many an innocuous and well-meaning individual who becomes possessed of power is transformed into a radically different type of human being. The feeling of power is intoxicating, and one loses his sense of proportion.

The chief concern of the world today should not be the destructive potentialities of nuclear fission, but rather the training of individuals in the righteous use of power. Wisely did the sages of Israel say, "Greater is he who governs his spirit than he who conquers a city."

Thus saith the Lord, "Let not the wise man glory in his wisdom, neither let the mighty man glory in his might, let not the rich man glory in his riches." (Jeremiah 9:22)

Lord, keep us humble.

We have probed deeply into the secrets of the universe and have discovered how to put the materials of nature at man's service. We have succeeded in annihilating distance and have brought into close proximity the widely separated parts of the globe. In seeming defiance of the basic laws of the world, we have learned to be borne on eagles' wings in celestial caravans. We boast of our conquest of the forces of nature and have become supremely self-assured. And, suddenly, man's most artful plans are rendered useless, and havoc and devastation descend upon earth, bringing death to scores and a trail of inconsolable heartache to their surviving families.

Lord, keep us modest.

Living in a land which is technically advanced and economically aggressive, we have achieved a high measure of material prosperity. We multiply acquisitions and point with pride to our possessions. We are certain that our needs are amply provided for and that we will be able to transmit a sizeable fortune to those who come after us. We become complacent, extremely pleased with our achievements and self-satisfied. And then, a sudden turn of fortune robs us of our security, and we stand bewildered before the debris of our vaunted wealth.

Lord, make us meek.

In the pursuit of our daily tasks, we feel the surge of vibrant life within us. Others may become ill and fall by the wayside, but we are strong. Death passes us by, although sometimes we may hear nearby the swish of his garments as he pursues his macabre work. We become smug and possessed by a feeling of well-being. We know that death is inevitable, but we are sure that so far as we are concerned, its advent is in the very distant future. And then we are stricken with a hopeless, debilitating illness which lays us low or are completely undone by the Grim Reaper who, in an instant, robs us of the breath of life.

In wisdom, in fortune or in health, may we never be arrogant.

O Lord, keep us humble.

To sympathize with the sufferings of others is a natural human instinct. There are few, if any, human beings who are not at some time deeply moved by the sight or the report of human misery. Reason and logic do not enter into the situation. The great majority of people do not ask whether helping one in need is socially constructive or individually uplifting. We are touched emotionally and we give. We are stirred by suffering and we vicariously suffer with the afflicted one.

This was demonstrated recently when a man who was digging a well was entombed in a pit under a garage. For twenty-seven hours, dozens worked, hundreds watched, and thousands prayed that the unfortunate man might be rescued alive. The story held the front page of our daily press. The man was dead when he was finally extricated and everyone felt moved by the failure to save this life. This testifies to the divine instinct of pity that resides in the hearts of human beings.

But it is rather strange that while the desperate plight of one human being evokes sympathy, the misfortunes of many do not call forth the same response. One might imagine that the pity for many would be the multiplication many times of the sympathy for one. This is not so. Do people have the same feeling of pity for a whole people as they have for an individual? Does the condition of our brethren in the transit camps in Israel evoke the same amount of sympathy as the plight of the well-digger? Do we feel as deeply the tragedy of the Chinese people as we do that of the cripple who sells pencils on the busy thoroughfare?

Evidently human nature is changed when it is dealing with large numbers of people. What a person would never dream of doing by himself seems perfectly right when that person is part of a mob. The crowd is not merely the total of people who compose it because the mob has a psychology of its own.

Being upright and sympathetic means having the ability to sympathize with the many as well as with the individual. But this point of view is far from being accepted. In our world, unfortunately, general life takes on the attitude of the business world, that wholesale is cheaper than retail—even in human life.

It was never intended that man should be alone. Built into the personality of every human being is the need for another, the imperious demand to break out of the confining limits of ourselves and to ally ourselves, in some manner, with other people. It is this which impels individuals to share their joys with and to communicate their problems and sorrows to others. What can be achieved by unburdening ourselves of our problems, by telling them to someone else, is of secondary importance. The primary consideration is to have the opportunity of lifting a heavy load off our shoulders and thus making lighter the anxiety that comes from having to bear the weight of a problem alone.

In the course of my daily tasks, I have occasion to listen to the problems of many people, young and old. I would be deceiving myself if I believed that anything I say to these troubled men and women constitutes a solution of their difficulties. But I am convinced that they feel better for having poured out their hearts to another person. Serious emotional problems should be handled by one professionally trained for that purpose. However, the small but troubling cares that gnaw at the hearts of people need only the sympathetic ear and the understanding heart.

I find that there are many whose difficulties arise from the fact that their view of a situation is out of focus. Trivial irritations are magnified beyond all proportion. A word spoken in haste, an unintended slight becomes the basis of bitter hatred. Sometimes people are disillusioned because life does not come up to their unrealistic notions. And then there are those who are unable or unwilling to accept defeat or grief and who would want life to be an uninterrupted series of pleasant events.

Many of the problems of life would be easier to endure, if not to solve, if mature people would but realize that tragedy is an integral part of human existence and that what counts is not whether sorrow enters our lives but, rather, the manner in which we face it. The dignity of man is displayed in the manner in which he accepts adversity.

If we can listen to the things that burden others and can encourage them to bear affliction bravely, to face life realistically, and to find worthwhile aspects even of an imperfect life, then we are performing a most useful function and can rest assured that we are contributing substantially to human welfare.

If we were asked to put our finger upon the major spiritual ailment of human beings today, I am sure that there would be many different answers. Some see the greatest problem in the preoccupation of human beings with the material things of life to the exclusion of every spiritual consideration. Others would answer that the pugnacious instinct in human nature is keeping the world in a turmoil. Still others feel that jealousy, individual and national, is the root of all the evils of the world. There is one thing all these opinions have in common, the assumption that our difficulties are based upon an erroneous philosophy of life.

May I be bold enough to suggest still another answer that differs from those mentioned above. I feel that our problems arise not from thinking along one line or another, but rather from not thinking at all. As I see it, the great difficulty is that most human beings are smug and complacent, completely satisfied with themselves and wholly approving of their own mode of life.

Observe the attitude of people you know and notice the smugness of their existence. The members of a family that is financially secure too frequently develop a patronizing attitude toward other people. You cannot convince these smug individuals that there is anything wrong with their way of life. I have heard them talk. They will discuss a subject giving the opinion of others and then they add, "But I say, etc. . . ." This, they feel, clinches the argument. They insist on telling you how things are done in their home.

Are such people disturbed by the plight of others? Are they touched by the suffering of human beings around them? They are, in a measure, and their response is a formal gesture of cooperation in philanthropic work. They let others do the hard, and often thankless work, while they content themselves with buying a ticket or writing a small check. Such people feel that by paying something above the price of a theatre ticket, they are discharging their obligations to society.

Let this not be misunderstood. We find no fault with people who support communal projects in any way. We resent the attitude of smug people who do nothing for Jewish and general philanthropic work except buy tickets. Such an attitude cannot by any stretch of the imagination lead to a vital Jewish life. To be a Jew means more than to write checks and to attend dinners.

The unprovoked attack by a group of Negro youths upon students of the Hasidic Lubavitcher Yeshivah is an event whose implications reach far beyond the boundaries of that institution. The incident in itself, the attack with broken bottles and chains upon Jewish youngsters who are as far removed from fighting and gang activities as any group could be, is sufficiently deplorable. But what such a demonstration bodes for the future is really frightening.

Gang fights are, alas! not strange phenomena in our city. But when the assailants shout anti-Semitic slogans and tell Jews that they don't belong in a community in the city, then the matter needs careful investigation.

Did these Negro boys become anti-Jewish as a result of their own thinking? Is it not rather true that they have taken over this attitude from their parents? Is it not the result of the teachings of a Malcolm X or a Lomax who do not recognize in us their most understanding fellow-citizens? For, in every age the Jew has stood in the forefront of every liberal movement, a result of the prophetic passion for social justice that we have inherited.

And, if oppression and centuries of social ostracism have taught us Jews anything, it is to be kind to others who suffer. We were admonished not to hate Egyptians, who had enslaved our ancestors for centuries because we had dwelled in their midst. Those who have suffered should feel most the need of not inflicting suffering on others.

I hear the answer to my observations. The Negro has suffered and still suffers from discrimination, a lack of equal opportunity with his white brothers, a wanton disregard of rights guaranteed to him by our Constitution, a failure to treat him with the consideration which every human being deserves. Much needs to be done and soon, too, to try to accord to Negroes, as well as others, the rights of American citizens.

16

However, this does not mean that we must overlook every reckless, lawless, wild act on the part of "stall-in" leaders and assorted Negro demagogues, and permit the life of decent, sympathetic citizens to be disrupted because of grievances. Even men of good will are fed up with the endeavor of some well-meaning but misguided people who are ready to condone the hooliganism and total irresponsibility of wrongdoers on the ground of unequal opportunity, or lack of playgrounds, or poor schools. Perhaps there has been a little too much coddling, perhaps we have been guilty of a little too much "understanding." Those of us who grew up in the ghetto, in Brownsville, or the East Side, or some other part of the city, learned that we must be law-abiding, and that if we violated the law, then punishment was inevitable.

If the Negroes who are struggling for equal rights want the support and efforts of other Americans, (and they are entitled to receive them from us), if they want us all to fight against civil-rights filibusters which are a blot on the record of America, then they must be prepared to think of the rights of others. I, for one, have no desire to enthrone those who will imitate the bad example of their oppressors. I want to be sure that we will get no hurts from those who are in the driver's seat.

There are certain traits and attitudes that human beings have acquired in the dawn of civilization and which persist, often unconsciously, despite all changes in the world. I have in mind specifically the habit of regarding the action of every inanimate object as coming from some person. Primitive man who stubbed his toe against a rock thought that there was a spirit in that rock which was responsible for his injury. We see this clearly in the attitude of young children who bump their heads against some object and then "spank" the object as if to punish the evil spirit in it. Unconsciously, sensible adults do the same thing.

All of us, I am sure, know at least one person who has refused to work in a great cause, be it a religious or a charitable one, because that person has been insulted or slighted by someone connected with the cause. The synagogue or the philanthropic organization becomes synonymous with some person in it, and we avenge ourselves upon the "evil spirit" in it. In Yiddish, there is a very graphic expression of this idea. Jews say of such a person as we have described that because he is angry at the cantor, he will not answer "Amen" after his blessings.

This whole matter may seem to be a trifling one, but in reality it is extremely important. It affects the work of many organizations, and it places a strain upon their leaders lest they offend some person by some unintentional act or word. But more important than this is the danger to society from human beings who have not shaken off their primitive ways, and who cannot distinguish between ideals and persons, between causes and their representatives. Democracy hasn't failed because we have some bigots in our midst. Religion is not bankrupt because some adherents to a particular group are unethical.

For Jews this thought is especially significant, because in spiritual matters we always felt the power of the ideal and excluded the personal element as much as possible. The name of our religion is not that of one of its founders. It is "Judaism" and not, for instance, "Mosaism." This, in itself, demonstrates the ability and the desire of the Jew to disentangle the personal element from the ideal of which some person happens to be the representative. If this distinction is clearly kept in mind, we shall rid ourselves as Jews and as human beings of the harmful vestige of primitive life.

Man is seeking to find an answer to a vexing problem. He wants to know why Jews, who are observant and perform all the ritual commandments of our faith, do not carry the religious attitude over into their relations with their fellowmen. He correctly indicates that one's attitude toward his neighbor and associates is the concern of Judaism as much as is the performance of *mitzvot*. He comes to the conclusion that what is lacking even in the most traditional schools is *yirat shomayim* (reverence of heaven). The solution he proposes is to call a conference of rabbis and Jewish educators to plan courses in religiously based ethics for our children.

There can be no doubt that much criticism of religion comes from the fact that there are people who are punctilious in ritual observance and careless in their ethics. If we examine the situation carefully, we will discover, I think, that this stems from a complete misunderstanding of Jewish law. It comes from the fact that unconsciously people treat Jewish religious observances as a system of magic. The feeling is that certain things must be done in order to produce desired results. There is so much concern with form that one completely loses sight of the substance. It is like going to the synagogue for services and then utilizing part of the time there to talk ill of someone. To divide the realm of the Lord from that of man, to say (as some do), "What belongs to the Lord is the Lord's and what belongs to man is man's" is completely to misinterpret the spirit of Judaism. One cannot be a "good" Jew and at the same time an unethical human being. The prophets of old denounced those Jews who brought sacrifices to the Temple and then continued their unethical practices. The Haftarah read on Yom Kippur morning should serve notice on every Jew that no prayer or observance is of any value unless it is accompanied by or results in better living.

Ceremonies are but the outer garments in which the ideals of religion clothe themselves. By themselves they are only expressions of what one hopes is an inner conviction. In the words of the psalmist, only he ascends the mountain of the Lord "who has clean hands and a pure heart."

The immediate effects of persecution upon a minority group are well known. Every one is familiar with the damaging and sometimes disastrous results that follow in the wake of discrimination, segregation, and physical attacks. But there is also a more remote effect all of these have upon the spirit of the persecuted. They develop fears and they begin to see everything through the spectacles of persecution. Whatever ill fortune they suffer is attributed to racial or religious hatred. While there is no doubt that bigotry is still too prevalent in our world, yet we must not see the spectre of prejudice where it does not exist.

All of us, I am sure, know of cases in which Jews have been denied employment or have failed to attain goals, which are in nowise attributable to anti-Semitism. This applies also to the Negroes who are the victims of discrimination, but who often see it where it does not exist. Two instances of this attitude have come to my attention.

A Negro family which purchased a home in a neighborhood where the renting of rooms is forbidden by a covenant in the deed, raised the issue of discrimination when an injunction was obtained to restrain them from renting rooms. It was proven beyond a doubt that similar action had been taken against white people who had violated the covenant. The second case is that of a group which made accusations against two Brooklyn hospitals. It was asserted in literature which was sent through the mail, that in several instances the hospitals refused to accept Negro children who died shortly thereafter. I investigated the situation and discovered that discrimination had absolutely nothing to do with the situation. Both of the hospitals have Negro nurses and employees, and a considerable number of their ward patients are Negroes. Yet the cry was raised that children were refused admittance because of racial discrimination.

Prejudice is a dreadful social malady and it causes untold misery in the world. However, it will not help if we are so fear-ridden that we see everything untoward as a manifestation of bigotry. It is even more unfortunate that there are some individuals and groups who exploit discontent for the achievement of some political goal. How sad it is to be persecuted, and how sadder still it is to have one's troubles used by others for selfish purposes. We must be bold in fighting prejudice, but our vision must not be blurred nor our minds warped as we set out to free the world from the blight of bigotry.

20

The highways are choked with traffic on Sundays, the children in school are restless, ice-cream vendors call prospective customers by means of bells, grown-ups appear on the street in adolescents' clothes, the tops of convertibles are down, the constant buzz of air conditioners is heard—summer is here. Young and old now look forward to a period of relaxation and rest. A year's work now comes to a close. I extend my hand to you, figuratively, and bid you a pleasant vacation, and, as I do so, it suddenly occurs to me what a shake of the hand expresses.

Hands may be used in many ways, and numerous expressions in our daily speech indicate their functions. To assist anyone is to "lend a hand," in which case the hand is a symbol of helpfulness and cooperation. If something is unimportant to us, we dismiss it with a wave of the hand. To share in an accomplishment is to "have a hand" in it. One who is domineering and autocratic is said to act in a "high-handed" manner, while he who is dishonest and uses unworthy methods to achieve a goal is called "underhanded."

Hands may be used to express love and sympathy and understanding. A clasp of the hand can be infinitely more expressive of our feelings toward another person than any number of words. The hand is likewise a weapon with which one can strike another human being. It functions as a ballot when, in taking a vote, the hand is upraised to denote approval or disapproval.

But to people who have lived within the influence of religion, the hands are used for prayer. The psalmist speaks of putting our hearts into our hands as we raise them in supplication. The hand is lifted up in the act of conferring a blessing upon another human being. It seems as if we want our hands to act as a sort of transmitter which will convey the deepest yearnings and most heartfelt wishes to others whom we love.

As the vacation period begins, I give you my hand, a token of the fact that you and I have worked together. I clasp your hand to express a feeling of kinship with all of you to whom it is my sacred and glorious privilege to minister. And I raise my hand and invoke upon you a blessing that the season of rest and relaxation may bring you health and joy and serenity of spirit.

Part of the unpleasant side of the rabbinate is the very frequent need of attending funerals and of endeavoring to bring some comfort to those who are bereaved. It is a difficult task, and even one who is a veteran in this calling finds his talents and powers taxed to the limit.

With the best of intentions, friends seek to bring consolation to the mourners. They sit with the saddened family before the funeral service and strive to strengthen a grieving husband or wife, parent or child, sister or brother, by calling attention to many irrelevant circumstances in the life of the deceased. Among the expressions I hear are "Well, that's life," or "We all have to die sometime," or "What can you do?" or "When your number is called, you have to go."

Sincere as all these statements are, they cannot reach the heart of the mourner. It would be well for all if Jews reread the advice of Rabbi Simeon ben Eleazar in the *Ethics of the Fathers.* He said, "Do not comfort your fellowman in the hour when his dead lies before him." Is it not true that in the hour of deepest grief one can express more to a friend by a warm handclasp and a sympathetic tear than through a meaningless, trite formula?

The perceptive Rabbi Simeon who gave advice on consolation likewise counseled his friends about another aspect of human relations: "Do not appease thy fellowman in the hour of his anger."

I have heard people complain that in attempting to make peace between two of their fellowmen, they have been abused and injured from both sides. This is often cited as a reason for an unwillingness to serve as a peacemaker. But it may be that the difficulty arises from the fact that the timing is poor. Perhaps much of the difficulty arises from failing to realize that there must be a cooling-off period before making overtures of peace. To try to pacify an individual when he is irate may serve only to intensify his anger. Some very placid, unemotional, neutral people don't know how one feels when he is very angry. The worst thing to do is to say to an angry friend, "Take it easy," "Calm down." The best thing to do is to wait until the bombs have ceased falling and then to argue reasonably.

Rabbi Simeon ben Eleazar has much to teach us.

HOLIDAYS and OBSERVANCES

We have been taught that we must put "first things first" in order to live intelligently, that is, we must establish a system of priorities. Every mature person must learn to put important matters before trifling or insignificant ones. This is not possible unless we know what is important and what is unimportant or less important. Jewish life suffers because many Jews concern themselves with minutiae at the expense of major Jewish principles. Examples of this attitude can be easily found.

A young man who was about to be married inquired of me whether his father had to attend the synagogue services on the Sabbath preceding the wedding when the prospective groom would be called to the Torah (*aufruf,* as it is known). When I asked why the parent couldn't be present, the young man answered that his father's business was such that Saturday was an important day. I told the prospective bridgroom that it was not imperative that his father attend the services. Then I wondered whether, by implication, I was giving the father a license to work on the Sabbath. I hastened to tell the questioner that he himself did not have to be at the services because the calling of the bridegroom is a practice that does not rank among the great obligations of Judaism. The incident made me think of others which revealed a woeful ignorance by Jews of the "first" which must be put at the head of the line.

A bride who is very much concerned about what kind of wedding band (gold or other metal, plain or engraved) is required by Jewish law, thinks nothing of violating the Sabbath by being "beautified" on that day. In fact, there is practically no requirement for any special kind of ring in Jewish law and furthermore one does not even have to use a ring. Similarly, the question is raised on which finger of which hand the wedding band is to be placed. This, at a wedding where the meal to be served is not kosher and the matter which is seriously considered is of no consequence whatsoever.

The celebration of a boy's becoming Bar Mitzvah is a striking illustration of the lack of a sense of priorities. It seems mandatory for most parents to have their son make his appearance in the synagogue, assemble the relatives and friends at the services, where many of them converse throughout the proceedings, and listen to a reading from the Prophets, whose words are unintelligible to the audience and the celebrant. But the Jewish learning to which every Jew is pledged practically from the cradle to the grave is totally forgotten.

When the "unveiling" or dedication of a tombstone takes place, it becomes a matter of serious concern to families, whereas the ideals by which the deceased lived are completely forgotten. It is a source of great surprise to most Jews when they learn that Jewish law makes no provision whatsoever for the unveiling of tombstones.

Thus it goes. The things that are essential are overlooked, and the trivia are scrupulously observed. This may be due to lack of knowledge, but there is also the possibility that it may come from the fact that it is easier to observe the unimportant than the significant portions of Jewish living, and a Jew can salve his conscience by substituting one for the other.

Two things are requisite for living one's life as a Jew: knowledge and honesty.

One of the great sources of difficulty in our contemporary society is to be found in the relationship of employer and employee. Life is made difficult, large numbers of people are inconvenienced, millions of dollars are lost almost daily, often there is physical harm and a threat to health as a result of labor disputes.

There can be no doubt that the organization of unions for the protection of the workers' welfare has brought significant improvement in the life of the toiler. The unsanitary conditions under which men worked, the long hours, the inadequate wages, the lack of consideration for the health of the worker and the employment of children at an early age—all of these have been infinitely improved and eliminated largely through union efforts.

But having said this, and at the risk of being called a reactionary or, perhaps, even a capitalist, I feel that it is necessary to call attention to the Jewish attitude towards work, which I see lacking as I look around me.

For a Jew, work was honorable. Even the diligent study of Torah did not excuse him from engaging in some occupation. Almost all the sages of the Talmud had some trade at which they toiled. Worship and work are both described by the same Hebrew word, *avodah*.

This dignity and nobility of labor need to be emphasized at a time when great energy is spent, not upon work, but upon an attempt to escape from it. For many, the important element in a work contract is how many days off it allows. Children in school who attend regular sessions work from about nine in the morning to twelve noon without refreshments. Yet grown people, some of whom come to work late quite regularly, seem not to be able to work for three hours without a coffee break or breaks. The numerous holidays which are part of the worker's schedule are

27

not so much a result of a need for recreation as the dislike for sustained labor. How else can one explain the fact that in some industries a worker is entitled to take a day off with pay to celebrate his or her birthday?

And that people do not like to work can be seen from how they act when they are at work. Inefficiency and sloppy procedures are evident everywhere. All around us we hear people say that you cannot expect satisfactory performance from any employee. Telephone operators, sales clerks, mechanics, bus drivers, office employees—many, too many of them display a lack of interest in what they are doing and are careless in their tasks and even surly in their attitude toward people.

I recognize that the organization and division of labor in our society is such that a great deal of the work which people have to perform is monotonous. But this is something that is an economic or social hazard invoked in life in a complex society. Maimonides says that the great men of the Bible "gave themselves willingly and reverently to the humblest tasks—to tilling the soil, to keeping sheep, to ordering their households—because they saw in them the path by which to approach God."

We must by all means strive to raise the standard of living for all people. We must provide recreation and rest for those who toil. But we must also learn the dignity of work and the moral obligation to give a day's work for a day's pay. Even in the Garden of Eden, we are told, Adam was not allowed merely to enjoy the fruit there. He was put there, in the words of the Bible, "to till it and to guard it." This lesson, I think, needs to be taught particularly to our children, many of whom do not have an adequate respect for the nobility or even the need of work.

More than usual interest should be shown in the discussions which took place at the recent convention of the United Synagogue youth. The sessions gave young people, including members of Atid (the college group of Conservative Judaism) an opportunity to discuss their grievances against the synagogue and the reasons for the alienation of young people from it. There is much justification in some of the criticism, but there is also a measure of irresponsibility.

That the synagogue has not yet done its task adequately in the field of social action cannot be denied. There are altogether too many members in our congregations who feel that we have no right to concern ourselves with the problems of civil rights, of poverty or of peace. Such matters are considered "politics;" and, it is asserted, the synagogue should deal only with "religion."

Perhaps it is this very distinction which is largely responsible for the dishonesty and the corruption of office-holders. Perhaps it is a forgetfulness of the biblical command that the king (or ruler) must write for himself a *Sefer Torah* and govern by its precepts. It is precisely because the domain of politics has been removed from the field of ethics, that we continue to have public scandals.

What is the purpose of the observance of *mitzvot*, the scrupulous carrying out of ritual practices? Are they to be regarded as magical instruments for receiving divine favor? In a comment on a verse in Psalms, the rabbis of old say that the purpose of the *mitzvot*, was to refine the character of man, to make him more sensitive. Nothing, therefore, which helps to improve the lot of our fellowmen is excluded from the purview of religion. Is it not our religious teachings which prompt us to aid Federation, with its program for the aged, the sick, the poor, and the underprivileged? Nor does Jewish law make skin color a test for benevolence. To the extent that we fail to stand with those who fight the ills of the world, we have not fulfilled our duty as Jews. In saying this, our young people are right.

But it is not true that we have failed completely to take a stand on these matters. A considerable number of our rabbis and outstanding religious leaders have been actively identified with the struggle for human rights. Congregations have given their facilities to "freedom schools," and United Synagogue affiliates have been asked to do business only with firms which do not discriminate against any minority groups in employment. Some of our young people who work in slums prefer to do so under the banner of some nondenominational group because somehow this seems more "broad-minded" or "liberal" to them.

The usual criticism that congregational leaders spend large sums on lavish buildings is tiresome. Some young people said that the edifices are used only three days a year. From my own experience, I know of few synagogue structures that are not used throughout the year. Besides, most of the youthful critics want a building with many conveniences, like an attractive ball-room for dancing and a gymnasium.

We must not make the mistake of equating Judaism with some kind of ethical culture or pale humanitarianism. To propose, as one student did, that we build small edifices and give the money collected for building purposes to some poverty program is unrealistic. For one thing, we do not know to whom to entrust such money, and the federal and state governments have not yet learned this either. But we must remember also that the average Jew does not contribute to a synagogue, and those who do, expect (and have a right to expect), that besides fighting economic poverty, the synagogue will also struggle against spiritual poverty.

It is the constant aim of rabbis (and clergymen generally) to bring their congregants to public worship. One cannot possibly criticize people who come to the synagogue to pray, although one may devoutly wish that such visits were more frequent. I do not chastise members for being "periodic" Jews. It is my conviction that if a Jew is sufficiently motivated by a Jewish holy day or festival to come to the synagogue, it is adequate proof that he considers himself part of of the religious Jewish community.

However, this does not mean that I can approve of what many people do after they have come to services. The manner in which many worshippers deport themselves in the synagogue leaves much to be desired. From where I stand I can see and hear much that distresses me, not only because it is a personal irritant, but also because it violates the rules laid down in Jewish law for conduct in a house of worship.

That people will come in at different times during the service is to be expected; that they should greet their friends is but natural. This, however, does not mean that people should engage in long conversation with some whom they have not seen for a long time. Incidentally, this is a valid reason for attending services weekly because the accumulation of news in seven days will not provide enough *"shmoos"* material for a long conversation. It is not like an annual report.

Jewish law admonishes the Jew to be aware of the reverence due to a House of God. In many synagogues there is inscribed over the Ark the sentence, "Know before Whom you stand." During the reading of the Torah, absolute silence by the congregation is required by Jewish law. And perhaps a very good insight into standards of action in the synagogue is the provision that one must not even kiss children there because the mind should be occupied with the love of God alone.

Even if one could condone conversation and noise on the ground that people were talking about sacred matters, discussing the Torah reading, I would have to be convinced that this is the subject of the constant, irritating talk during services. Our people are not the greatest offenders in this matter, but we pride ourselves on setting standards for others.

Merely to come to the synagogue in fulfillment of a social obligation (it's the right thing to do) is to make a mockery of our religious faith; and one can hear Isaiah's words to his contemporaries when they came to the Temple, "Who asked this of you?"

True prayer is possible only in a quiet atmosphere, when contemplation turns our hearts to God. The atmosphere of the market place or the spirit of a class reunion in the synagogue is contrary to Jewish law. The synagogue service must not be allowed to become a liturgical coffee klatsch.

It is just a store which I have passed literally hundreds of times, of the kind with which we are amply supplied. But, last week, the words on the sign in the window awakened thoughts in me completely foreign to their real meaning. The sign advertised the services performed by the establishment, viz., pressing, cleaning, repairing, and dyeing. This work is done on the clothes we wear, and I realized it can also be done on our inner selves.

A certain amount of pressing is an essential ingredient in life. While all of us would prefer a life without pressure, yet we must recognize that there is undeniable value in the difficulties and hardships which life brings to us. In life, as in the tailor's shop, pressing is necessary to put us into shape. The rabbis of old compared the Jewish people to the olive. They say that just as the olive does not yield its oil until it is pressed, so the noblest qualities of the Jew become manifest only through pressure.

Like clothes, we also need periodic cleaning. Even with most noble intentions, a certain amount of the spiritual grime and dust is bound to adhere to us. Unconsciously we take over from the environment standards and habits of which, initially, we completely disapprove. It becomes necessary that, from time to time, we should examine ourselves and, discovering some stain on our personality, cleanse ourselves of it. The annual occasion for this process is Yom Kippur, of which the Bible specifically says that it is intended for cleansing purposes. However, one need not wait for the great Atonement Day but can utilize any day or any spare moment for stain removing.

The third service we can render ourselves is repairing. "To err is human, said a great poet, and all of us know of the mistakes we make, of the offense we give to the sensibilities of others, of our disregard of their rights, of our failure to do our duty. Regret for the errors we've made is not enough unless, with it, there is a determined effort to repair the harm that has been done to ourselves, as well as to others.

But there is one other process to which life is subjected, that is, dying. The contemplation of death affects human beings in different ways. For some, the realization of its inevitability leads to utter despair. To others, it is the justification for seizing as much of life's pleasures as possible since one doesn't know when death will call. But for some, it means the determination to accomplish what is worthwhile, something which will, in a way, extend life even after its course has been run. It is true that the tailor advertised "dyeing" and not "dying," but our contemplation of death colors our outlook on life, the realization that we must die helps to dye our fundamental philosophy.

Pressing, cleaning, repairing, and dyeing—important services rendered by life's tailor shop.

If all people were conscious of the foundations upon which our civilization rests, they would pause and universally celebrate a great event. The city of Jerusalem is 3,000 years old, and this fact should be the occasion for a worldwide birthday celebration.

No city in the world is as spiritually significant or as historically important as this one. It is sacred to three of the great religions of the world, Judaism, Christianity, and Islam. It is sanctified by the precious memories which cling to it and by the blood shed in its defense. For Jews, the city of Jerusalem represents the great vital center of our faith and it occupies a most important spot in the hopes of our people for the future.

When King David captured the city and established his country's capital there 3,000 years ago, there began a long and soul-stirring epic. It was here that King Solomon built the Temple which became the central sanctuary of the Jewish people. Even when far removed from the land of his origin, the Jew was commanded to turn east in prayer, so that he might look toward Jerusalem. There, according to tradition, Abraham was prepared to sacrifice his son to prove his loyalty to the Lord. The Mishnah contains a beautiful description of the rites which were associated with the pilgrimages to the holy city which Jews made on Pesach, Shevuot, and Succot.

The Temple was destroyed and many Jews were carried into Babylonia as captives. There they vowed never to forget Jerusalem, and they never forgot. Its name was in their prayers, in their hearts at all times. But there lay ahead a long period of suffering and hardship. The Maccabees wrested it from the Syrians only to hold it until Rome conquered it and laid it waste. The period of exile then began for the Jewish people. Every year on the Ninth of Ab, the day that marked the destruction of the First and Second Temples, Jews mourned the loss of the city and the dissolution of Jewish national life. But with the lament was coupled the undying hope that the city would be rebuilt and Jews would rejoice there again. This had been promised by the prophets; Isaiah and Amos foretold it.

Much was destined to happen before the hope would be realized. Almost every nation of ancient times and many in the Middle Ages struggled for possession of the city. There was the period of the Crusades, with its bloody battles for the city. But through it all, the Jews continued to hope. More and more of them came back to the ancient city. They kissed its soil and worshipped there exultantly.

Finally after a long period of praying, hoping, struggling, and working, the state of Israel was established. In the face of much opposition, the capital of the Jewish state has come home once again to Jerusalem, and we pray that Isaiah's words may be fulfilled:

For out of Zion shall go forth the Law
And the word of the Lord from Jerusalem

Great truths are often expressed in simple words and by humble people, and we submit here a gem which fell from the lips of a little boy in our religious school.

The teacher was discussing what she called "positive" and "negative" Jews, when she asked, "Does anyone know what a 'negative' Jew is?" Several hands were raised, and our little philosopher, called on for his opinion, answered, "I'm not sure but I think it's something like in photography. A negative is something, a picture, but it has to be developed."

Here, in a brief sentence, a great truth was expressed. The boy, a youngster of ten, was right. A negative Jew is one who needs to be developed. For the problem in American Jewish life today is exactly that. The basic meaning of the world "develop" is to unroll or unfold, to make active that which is latent.

The problem with which we are faced in our work is not that of making people Jewish. If we had to do that, we might find ourselves powerless. Fortunately for us, we do not have to begin from the beginning. We have something on which to build. Who is the Jew who does not remember an old mother or grandmother who read from a little book with yellowing pages some mysterious prayers? Where is the man or woman who does not recall a mother waving her hands over Sabbath candles in some mysterious fashion? Is there a person who does not recall a visit to the synagogue with his or her parents? Can we find a Jew who has completely forgotten the sweet odors of those strange foods which were prepared by a pious mother? In brief, we have something to start with in the heart of every Jew, but it needs to be developed.

What our little friend who defined the negative Jew failed to realize was that negatives are always developed in dark rooms, and the analogy carries over into Jewish life. It is unfortunate that darkness brings out the positive in Jewish life, that the development cannot take place under conditions of light and joy. Perhaps that comes from the fact that under the stress of difficulty and misfortune we are more likely to take stock of ourselves, to place in their true perspective the things which are important and those which are trifling.

We shall continue to try to develop the latent potentialities of Jews, to endeavor to nurture even the vestigial portions of Judaism which still remain in Jewish hearts. We can do this if we are helped in our efforts by those who want to transform their negatives into positives, so as to reveal a true picture of Jewish life.

What does one do to attract Jews to the synagogue? This has become an important question in our time when our people have lost the habit of praying. Since the fundamental motivation for synagogue attendance has been lost, we are naturally forced to look for methods of "attracting" people to services.

One way is to increase the number of social functions such as card parties, dances and entertainments. Even dances could be Jewishly motivated if they were arranged in connection with Jewish holidays like Purim or Hanukah. But one finds it hard to understand what place a Halloween or New Year's Eve dance can occupy in the schedule of a synagogue's activities.

There is another device for getting seat-warmers (they're not worshippers) into the synagogue. One can arrange "specialty" nights on Friday evenings. Thus, congregations arrange Masonic nights, Boy and Girl Scout nights, Kiwanis nights, and many others.

Sometimes a service is made "attractive" by arranging for some politician to deliver the address or by having a raconteur tell a series of humorous stories.

Last week, however, I discovered a novel way of getting Jews into the synagogue. It came in the form of an announcement on a synagogue bulletin board in front of an edifice allegedly dedicated to worship and study. In big letters there appeared the following: "Davy Crockett Night" and then lower down, "Roy Campanella in person."

Here is a congregation for which we must have respect, a congregation with a spark of originality. After all, if heads must be covered at a traditional service, why not substitute a coonskin cap for a yarmulke? As a matter of fact, the distinguished European rabbis of the past used to wear fur-trimmed hats. And since Davy Crockett helped to push back the frontier, perhaps he can be used

38

as a symbol of the pioneers who have built and are building the land of Israel.

But I find it hard to understand what Roy Campanella can symbolize, in spite of my respect for him as a professional baseball catcher (perhaps the best in his field) and as an effective batsman. Since, as a catcher, he must always be at "home," it would seem that he is a decidedly inappropriate symbol for any effort to bring Jews to the synagogue. The trouble in Jewish life is that we already have too many "catchers," people who do nothing but receive what others give. We need more "pitchers" in congregations, people who will give as well as receive.

These are musings on the ways of synagogue life in America. If the rabbi needs an audience to which to preach, if we want to fill our synagogues, we have a new method to achieve our purpose, viz., a "Davy Crockett night" with "Roy Campanella in person."

The world we live in puts a premium upon inventions, the discovery of new techniques and gadgets. But the piling up of labor- and time-saving devices has not measurably increased human happiness. Perhaps instead of trying new methods and ideas it might be wise to bring out some of the old ones and to find in them the clue to inner tranquility. We who have discovered beauty in antiques should be able to find suggestions for living in institutions and practices which so many have discarded.

It cannot be denied that life today is characterized for most people by strains and tensions. Medical research has indicated how this situation results not only in mental disturbances but also in physical ailments. It is extremely interesting to note that Jews of an older generation did not suffer, to the extent that we today do, from various organic diseases. What shall we do?

I want to suggest something unbelievably simple—a return to the observance of the Sabbath in the traditional way. As an argument I want to leave out the strictly religious reasons for the observance. Nor do I want to base it upon what the Sabbath has meant in the preservation of the people of Israel. It is rather my purpose to point out the therapeutic value of the Sabbath.

It gave to the Jewish housewife and mother a complete day of relaxation, free from the routine of daily tasks. There was no shopping, no cooking, and none of the other many tasks which a woman performs. Members of the family came to know one another. The meals meant more than the consumption of food. The home looked more beautiful, and the songs that were sung at the table provided a pleasant setting for a meal which tasted different from those that were hastily devoured during the week by the harassed businessman. The father had the opportunity of talking to his children and of checking on the progress in their studies.

40

The services in the synagogue provided an opportunity for public worship, but also enabled the Jew to meet his friends, to listen to the words of the Torah, and to get instruction through the sermon on the problems that agitated the Jewish community.

But what was perhaps most important was a relaxation of the tension under which the Jew lived throughout the week. The mind was completely devoid of any thought of business. The really devout Jew did not merely absent himself from his office on the Sabbath but also kept every thought of it far from him. For at least twenty-four hours there was tranquility of spirit and peace of mind. The Sabbath was like a refreshing bath which removed the impurities of the work-day week. The observant Jew was a happy, healthy, normal human being.

I suggest, therefore, that more Jews try Sabbath observance as a remedy for distress and tension. Let us bring back the traditional observance of the Sabbath and thus help in the purging of neuroses and complexes. It is worth trying.

The growth of large cities has created some of the most difficult problems of our time. But, in addition to the positive evils of slums, air pollution, traffic tie-ups, and mass transportation difficulties, there is another evil in urbanization, that of being removed from nature. In our large urban centers, we have lost the thrill of seeing the first flowers in the spring, the awakening of the trees from their winter slumber, the chirping of the birds, the fragrance of flowers, the springy turf beneath our feet.

We erect *succot* to remind us that our ancestors dwelt in booths when they traveled through the wilderness. By the four species we are reminded of the harvest season and of our dependence upon God and natural forces. But aside from all of these historic and religious considerations, Succot should afford us an annual weekly respite from the turmoil, the haste, the pressures of daily city living and turn our hearts and minds to those things that remain with us always. This is extremely important in an era when there is an almost inescapable tendency to look for something new and different in every area of life, in clothes, music, art, literature, and gadgets. We need to be made conscious of the serenity which comes from being close to nature, after all the artificiality which is so much a part of our lives.

In ancient times our people was commanded, while laying siege to a city, not to destroy its trees. "For is the tree of the field man that you should besiege it?"—thus reads the translation in our texts, but literally it reads, "For man is the tree of the field."

Like trees, we have the ability to provide welcome shade for those who are scorched by the heat of afflictions and fears. Like trees, we can provide nourishment by the fruit of our actions to those who hunger. Like trees, we can make our influence felt without being on the move. We can stand in one spot and let our influence reach out beyond us. Like trees, we can make sure that even after we ourselves are no longer young and fresh, there will remain a stock and root from which renewed life can spring forth. Perhaps also we can see in ourselves at least some qualities of the Torah, which has most appropriately been called, the Tree of Life.

Succot is a festival of joy, a holiday which, after the sombre penitential season, brings to us the joy of living and the contentment and tranquility which come from recognizing our kinship with nature.

One of the unique institutions of Judaism is the period called "The Ten Days of Penitence" between Rosh Hashanah and Yom Kippur. None of the other religious systems of which I know anything provides a specific period for self-scrutiny during the year and a chance to alter the direction of our lives. To achieve this goal, several steps are necessary.

The first thing one must do is to *recall*. It is necessary to bring into the forefront of our minds an inventory of the wrongs we have committed and of the good we have left undone. Perhaps a single act may not stand out in our minds, but when seen in the content of a year's activity, it assumes a different appearance.

Next we must *restore* the things we've damaged and the people we have hurt. Often we fail to realize how much harm we do by injuring another person's image of himself. What I think of another human being is not half as important as what he thinks of himself. To tear down another's idea of himself is to violate what is his most precious possession.

We are then called upon to *relent,* to give up our hatred of others, to cease from the seemingly small yet actually large acts of persecution of our fellowmen, whom we wound by insults and oppress by prejudice. It may confer a certain self-satisfaction to wreak revenge upon someone, but it harms others end spiritually devastates ourselves.

The next step is to *repent,* to feel sincerely sorry for misdeeds of commission and even more, perhaps for the sins of omission. There cannot be any use in this period of solemn contemplation unless it produces the feeling of sincere regret for the misuse of our time, our talents, and our treasure.

And finally we must *resolve,* with a complete consciousness of obstacles in the way of fulfilling our noblest ambitions, we must determine that the New Year which lies ahead challenges us to struggle against hardships, to endure frustrations, to suffer defeat, to experience pain but yet to have the determination to make our lives better than they have been.

The cry of rebellious college students is a call for "restructuring the university." Rosh Hashanah demands the restructuring of our inner universe.

Rebellion is the first sign of a desire for freedom. The child who refuses to do what the teacher asks and meets every request or order with a "No," is endeavoring to assert its freedom. This spirit of rebellion we carry with us into our mature lives and it is a valuable asset. But it has value only if it is regarded as merely the first step in the achievement of personal freedom. If it should remain the only mark of freedom, it will not produce any beneficial effects.

Frequently I become involved, against my will, in an argument about Judaism. A person will say, "I don't believe" something or other. Then there ensues a rather heated denunciation of some Jewish practice or belief. Sometimes I cannot be uncivil enough to ask, "Now that I know what you don't believe, perhaps you will tell me what you do believe." The question might stun the self-assured rebel. He might find it very hard to describe his positive convictions as clearly as he does his negative criticisms. As a matter of fact, it often happens that people resort to negative criticism in order to avoid the need for formulating a positive program.

I spoke to a man during this past week whose conversation suggests the foregoing observations. He prided himself on the fact that he was a "free" thinker. He had come to certain conclusions many years ago and he clung to them tenaciously. To me it seemed that he was denying himself the freedom to change his mind. Despite his alleged freedom, he was chained to a certain pattern of thought.

To destroy, to pull down is a desirable thing only if it means preparation for something to be built. There is no virtue in denial per se, and the ability to criticize is not a mark of intellectual superiority. It is understandable that there should be ideas to which we cannot subscribe, but one cannot base a philosophy of living upon a continued negation.

There may be certain aspects of Jewish practice and belief which do not appeal to some. They have a perfect right to question the validity of these things. But nothing will be achieved by an almost belligerent "No," unless there is something positive which one can maintain. Rebellion against what is, must be only a prelude to that which we feel ought to be.

44

A little boy about eight years old came into my office at the suggestion of his teacher, to get my decision on a religious matter. The subject of his inquiry can be stated briefly. He has worn his skull cap until it is no longer serviceable and he wants to know what a Jew should do with an "emeritus" skull cap. In his mind was no doubt the idea that just as one must dispose of sacred books and objects in a specified fashion, so also his *yarmulke* or *kippah* must be reverently treated.

It would be difficult, I felt, to explain to this little boy the idea that his skull cap had no innate sanctity. It might even shock him to learn that the head covering which is bound up in his mind with prayers and Torah study, has no intrinsic holiness. I told this boy that he should put the skull cap aside and keep it so that in future years he could look at it and remember that he used it to begin his study of Torah.

Heartening as it is to see a little boy who is concerned about the sanctity attached to an object, yet I ask myself whether, in his future life, this youngster will appreciate the holiness of those things which for us, as Jews, are truly consecrated. Is it not true that a large portion of our people attribute sanctity to minutiae, to what are often nothing but accumulated superstitions, and fail in their respect of what is essential? When may one visit a cemetery after the death of a loved one? May the shoes of the deceased be given away? May one name the baby after a certain person? May the groom or bride walk with this or that one? These are the matters which trouble Jews, while Sabbath observance, regular worship, study—these are neglected. It is my hope that as my little friend grows up he will be concerned as much with the *t'philin* on his head as he is with his worn-out skull cap.

One of the great disciplines the Torah teaches the Jew is the ability to make distinctions. In one of the most important sections of the Pentateuch, we are told that we must learn to distinguish between what is sacred and what is profane. If one were to ask what harm there can be in attributing a sacred quality to all things, we would answer by saying that investing the prosaic, profane things with holiness will lead to a failure to sanctify the things which deserve our reverence. Let little boys be concerned with an old skull cap, but let grown-ups be concerned with a still older Torah.

What is American Judaism like? The answer may be given in statistical studies or sociological research. But an easier method is to observe some isolated incident that conveys the answer in very graphic terms. I found it, for instance, on a sign in a store window on our local Main Street.

The emporium sells non-kosher meat, evidently to Jewish customers. The aforementioned sign bore the inscription, "Closed Thursday and Friday (Rosh Hashanah), open on Saturday." Here you have a picture of the approach of the average American Jew toward Judaism.

It can hardly be expected that I should underestimate the importance of the High Holy Days. They are intended to call the Jew to repentance, to an appraisal of his actions and to meditation on the important elements in human life. The appeal of these days is so great that only one who is totally untouched by Jewish feeling would neglect their observance.

Yet, historical truth compels us to note that in biblical times, Rosh Hashanah did not occupy the prominent place in the calendar of holidays that it holds among us. Aside from every other consideration involved in the evolution of this day as one of the most important ones of the year, there is also the fact that the failure of Jews to attend the synagogue regularly throughout the year makes this holiday stand out more prominently.

However, the Sabbath has, in every age, been one of the indispensable elements in Jewish life. It has provided a weekly opportunity for physical relaxation and spiritual renewal. It created an atmosphere in the home, through special foods, religious hymns (*zmirot*) and ennobling leisure which carried the Jew through the rest of the week. The Jewish mother was free from enslavement to shopping and cooking chores. She became "the woman of valor" described in the Book of Proverbs. Since travel was interdicted, the family remained together and the sense

46

of belonging was strengthened. The failure to observe the Sabbath in first, fashion has resulted in a falling off in synagogue attendance and the disappearance of all the home observances which gave strength to Jewish life.

The matter, however, goes deeper than this. The assignment of supreme importance to Rosh Hashanah is a striking illustration of the failure on the part of ill-informed Jews to distinguish between the more and the less important, to have an intelligent scale of values in thinking about Judaism. Many examples might be given of a disregard of essentials and a concern for things of lesser significance. Until and unless Jews learn to put first things first, we shall continue to confront a chaotic situation in the Jewish community. We will achieve nothing as long as we're "closed on Rosh Hashanah" and "open on Saturday."

From a strict point of view, Yom Kippur is the holiday which is more religious in its essence than any other which Jews celebrate. Let me make clear what this statement means.

Other festivals (except Rosh Hashanah), are connected with some memorable event or period in the life of the Jewish people. They have national significance and involve the life of the Jewish people as a group. Rosh Hashanah and Yom Kippur deal with the individual, the latter even more so than the former. On the most solemn day of the Jewish year, every person thinks in terms of the fundamental problems of life, of man's relation to his Maker, to himself, and to his fellowmen. Such subjects as the ultimate goal of life, the need for repentance, the urge to set oneself right with one's fellowmen—these matters agitate the heart of the Jew on Yom Kippur. It is the sort of religious observance which could be joined in even by a non-Jew because its content is universal in its appeal.

The feeling of repentance springs from a desire in sensible and sensitive people to make good their errors, to make their lives more noble than they have been. We feel the need for changes and we resolve to set ourselves with determination on the path to those needed changes and improvements. But how shall they be brought about? It seems to me that there are two conflicting opinions in this matter which are expressed in religion on the one hand and in sociology or economics on the other. The social sciences and philosophies feel that society and its institutions must be changed first, and if that is done, the individual will, as a result, become a better person since he will live in a milieu that permits him to be upright. The major problem from this point of view is the problem of remaking society. Religion, on the other hand, has always felt that there can be no change in society until there has been a change in the individual. It calls to every person to remake himself or herself, feeling that if human beings have a change of heart, then society will reflect the spirit of the units which compose it. In other words, religion wants to proceed from the inside out while the social philosophies want to proceed the other way.

There can be no doubt that these processes are mutually dependent upon one another. A righteous person will find it very difficult, if at all possible, to live a good life in an unrighteous society, and we must therefore strive to create the conditions which will enable good people to live. But it is the message of Yom Kippur that no elaborate scheme of social reconstruction will ever succeed unless we have first prepared people to implement it. If we do not experience a change of heart, then all efforts toward bettering the world are futile. This is the fundamental meaning of the ideal of *T'shuvah,* repentance, which is the basic idea underlying the observance of the most sacred day of the Jewish year.

Some words painted on the side of the truck of a general contractor called my attention to a problem which often faces many people.

In attempting to describe the services he renders, the truck owner said, "Violations removed" and "New heating systems installed." The first of these statements referred, of course, to the man's ability to repair defective equipment whose operation violated some city ordinance. But as I read the words they took on wider meaning.

Already in biblical times, an immortal writer said, "There is not a righteous person on earth who does good exclusively and does not sin." Even he who shuts himself away from the world in cloistered haunts, may sin through thoughts that assail his mind occasionally. The confession which we recite on Yom Kippur contains a catalog of potential, if not actual, violations of which we are guilty. For, we violate laws of our city or country, we violate the commandments of Judaism, and we violate what we know is noblest in us, for the sake of some momentary gain or advantage. All of these leave their impress upon us, and there comes a time when we suffer from a sense of guilt. We look for some power which can remove violations.

Religious people found and still find relief in a confession of wrong-doing. We realize that past violations cannot be removed, but we are convinced that we can guard against them in the future. Nothing is as effective as a periodic examination of ourselves, a pursuit for which most people do not seem to have any time.

But the past must never so affect our present life as to make the future a dismal one. Each one of us can get the second service which the aforementioned contractor offered. Spiritually, we can acquire a new heating system. We have it in our power to remake ourselves, to develop a new zeal and glow of enthusiasm for the things which make life richer and which will correspond to that which is noblest within us. In laymen's terms, in non-theological vocabulary, this is what it means to glimpse the face of the divine. We can re-create ourselves—that is the essence of our faith in man's dignity. Every one of us can, for ourselves, spiritually do the work which the general contractor offered to the public.

50

The ten days that intervene between Rosh Hashanah and Yom Kippur have for centuries been regarded as a period of repentance, an opportunity for introspection. According to a rabbinical tradition, Jews who are neither total sinners nor perfect saints, but just ordinary mortals, are given the chance during this period to make resolutions that will make them worthy of the blessings of the New Year.

If I were compiling a list of resolutions for the average Jew in our community, I think I would submit the following as the irreducible minimum. I would have every Jew say:

1) I resolve that in the coming year I shall attend services in the synagogue as often as I can because I recognize that Judaism without the Sabbath and prayer is not that for which our people has sacrificed so much.

2) I resolve that in the coming year I shall make my home Jewish by observing Jewish holidays there, by making my children regard the things they enjoy as heavenly blessings rather than rewards for merit.

3) I resolve that in the coming year I shall read at least several Jewish books and thus, as in other ways, keep myself informed of the life of my people.

4) I resolve that in the coming year I shall take a vital interest in and make sacrifices for my valiant sisters and brothers who are struggling to establish the state of Israel upon firm foundations.

5) I resolve that in the coming year I shall contribute to philanthropies in proportion to my means, uninfluenced by the niggardly giving of those Jews who evade their responsibilities.

6) I resolve that in the coming year I shall deal honestly with my fellowmen, recognizing that as a Jew I cannot do less. I shall also strive to make justice prevail in the world and shall do my share in aiding victims of discrimination and exploitation no matter who they may be.

7) I resolve that in the coming year I shall do my share in communal work and not find an excuse for inactivity in my personal disapproval of men or policies.

8) I resolve that in the coming year I shall live proudly as a Jew, refuting slanders against my people and living in such a way as to give the lie to any calumny directed against us.

9) I resolve that in the coming year I shall uphold American traditions and help make my country a leader on the road to international understanding and peace.

This may seem like a difficult program. In reality, it is nothing more than an affirmation of the principles of Judaism.

Festivals are the punctuation of the normal life of the Jew. For one who understands Judaism and takes its precepts seriously, holidays merely serve to emphasize the cardinal principles of our faith which should be a matter of daily concern to the Jew. Mature people realize that parties do not constitute the important part of life but are useful only to the extent that they underscore family relationship, milestones on life's journey, or feelings of friendship. Sensible people realize the futility of making of one's life a series of parties.

Yet, if one can judge from synagogue attendance, many grown-up Jews live in a "party" atmosphere. They come to the synagogue on the High Holy Days. They absorb at least some of the ideals which those days are intended to inculcate. Yet, only a few days afterward, they seem to live as if their next contact with the synagogue will be on the coming High Holy Days.

The best illustration of this attitude can be seen in the contrast between the attendance in the synagogue on Yom Kippur and on the Sabbath which follows it immediately. After Yom Kippur, we see empty seats once again staring us in the face; once more we see the faithful ones in their accustomed places. It is as though Rosh Hashanah and Yom Kippur had not been at all. What is left of all the sublime thoughts and the noble resolutions of the most sacred season of the year?

To the understanding Jew, every day is filled with occasions for thanksgiving, for meditation, for opportunities to put into practice the imperishable ideals so eloquently voiced by the prophets. There is nothing so commonplace but that it offers a chance to reveal our consciousness of the dignity and worthwhileness of life.

It is true that daily life is not as spectacular as are the festive days. The incessant round of duties, the routine that governs so much of our life is here again. But it is well to remember that this is life; the rest is the punctuation. Whether Jews are sincere in their devotions on the High Holy Days can best be ascertained by seeing how they act when those days are over. If the rest of the year is untouched by their influence, then we've celebrated in vain. We must realize that after the spiritual honeymoon we must settle down to the business of daily living.

At this season of the year which, for Jews, is associated with high religious ideals, almost every one who is a Jew gives some thought to the ultimate questions of life. As we celebrate the awe-inspiring holidays we are made aware of the problems that lie at the core of human existence. But the idea that recurs in our prayers, above all others, is repentance.

Jews, on Yom Kippur, recite a long confession of sins, and ask to be forgiven for them. Forgiveness, however, must be preceded by repentance, without which no atonement is possible.

It may be said that all of this is the concern of theologians, that the subject is one that has no significance for the average person. Yet a little reflection will make it abundantly clear that here is a matter that vitally affects the relations of people to each other, and nations in their attitudes toward other nations.

In essence, repentance means the ability to admit that one has made a mistake and is sorry for it. This is by no means an insignificant accomplishment, because we are prompted to defend what we say or do as being beyond all question. It demands self-discipline to be able to say, "I was wrong." All of us know people who are complacent, who are well satisfied with themselves, who are convinced that the manner in which they do things is correct in every way, who hate to have their faults pointed out to them. Once a year, at least, the Jew is expected to examine himself scrupulously and to discover the errors he has made.

In western Germany a reborn nation is beginning to emerge, anxious to take its place in the council of nations. There are many, particularly those in high places, who feel that Germany paid the penalty for militarism and for the atrocities which she committed. Certainly, any religious person would say that she ought to be given the opportunity to rebuild the shattered cities and lives of her people. But, for me, there remains an important question: Has Germany repented? Are her citizens honestly sorry for what they did? Do they admit their mistakes? I am not sure that I can give an affirmative answer to these questions. Prepared as I am to forgive, I must first be convinced that there has been *t'shuvah* (repentance).

"To err is human, to forgive, divine," but higher than the human and a little below the divine, stands repentance, the ability to say, "I have done wrong."

Ours is an age of restlessness. People are moving constantly and there seems to be a rebellion against becoming fixed or rooted in any place or within any group. Young people drop out of school, leave their families and go traveling, here or abroad, staying in various places for short periods of time. Anything that suggests permanence must be avoided.

The history of man's advance is the change from the life of the nomad to that of the settled tiller of the soil. The nomadic shepherds pitched tents at a fertile spot; and when the grazing animals had consumed the surrounding grass, they folded their tents and moved on. Evidently this urge to keep moving has remained with us. This is true, not only in our attitude to the physical environment, but also in our relations with human beings. Many young people live together without marriage because they do not want to make their relationship permanent. Frequently we hear the warnings of people admonishing us not to get "involved." This means that while an interest in people or social groups may be desirable, one must guard against making this interest a permanent matter.

The only unchanging thing in life, for most people, is change. Obsolescence is built into our machines and gadgets and we are encouraged to trade in the old for the new. This has nothing to do with improved techniques or devices. I speak here only of change for the sake of change. Yet as the French say, the more things change, the more do they remain the same. This is undoubtedly one of the great values of the Sabbath. It makes movement cease. It says, "Don't travel. Stay where you are. Don't run from one thing to another. Sit down and discover, beneath the constant changing events, the ideas over which neither time nor circumstance have any dominion."

It is typical of our time that one of the popular singing groups is called Rolling Stones. This describes the attitude of many young people toward life. The fact that such stones do not gather moss does not concern me (not all young people like moss), but one cannot erect a structure upon them until they stop rolling.

We have need of people who will sit still for a while, and thus give themselves a chance to discover who they are and what they really want. The Twenty-Third Psalm contains the formula of the meditative person: "He leads me beside the still waters." One cannot very well see himself in the rushing stream, but is mirrored only in the still waters.

54

Many and various are the sights I see "from where I stand." Consider for a moment this one, observed last Saturday. In the first row of the synagogue sat a lady who felt that her appearance needed some repairs. So she proceeded to extract a vanity case from her purse which she opened, and after gazing at herself in the mirror decided that she needed some powder on her nose. She applied it deftly and then surveyed her handiwork. A good job—she seemed content. Ah! but the lips needed some attention, too. She produced a lipstick and went to work at the job of lacquering her lips. This job done, she replaced her vanity case in her purse, evidently convinced that she was pleasing in the sight of God.

There is no question of morals involved in this situation. Cosmetics were invented for the purpose of beautifying the female of the species. But, in my humble opinion, it is decidedly bad taste to beautify oneself in the synagogue. Where is the subtle line of distinction that makes it ill-mannered for one to manicure her fingernails in the synagogue and perfectly proper to arrange one's face there?

I can see the wisdom of Jewish law prohibiting the carrying of a purse on the Sabbath. No purse, no vanity case. Besides, it may be of interest to note that Jewish law prohibits a Jew from looking into a mirror when he prays. But this doesn't apply to the lady in question because she wasn't praying. To see such things from the pulpit is distressing. Perhaps it is better, under such conditions, to be, paraphrasing the Bible and Huxley, "Eyeless in Midwood."

If one examines the Jewish calendar carefully, he will find that the arrangement of the festivals, during this month, falls into a very logical pattern. While it is true that seasonal and historical elements determined the sequence of the important holidays, yet one can find a plan in the order which commends itself to reason.

As a new year approaches, one thinks in terms of the past and the future. The present is forgotten. We think of the defeats and heartaches as well as of the achievements and joys of a year which has passed. We look ahead to another year with uncertainty mingled with hope. The perils that threaten the world and the slender thread of human life awaken within us the need to reach out for support and strength. This is Rosh Hashanah.

We realize that with all our best intentions, we have fallen short of the high ideals we profess and truly want to accomplish. We recognize that we have been harsh in our treatment of our fellowmen, that we have taken advantage of others for our personal gain, that we have been self-centered and arrogant. We cannot comfortably begin a new year with such matters on our conscience. We feel the need of setting ourselves straight with God and our fellowmen. This process takes place on Yom Kippur.

If one has properly appreciated the meaning of the Solemn Days, and if one has truly meditated and atoned, then one should be able to rejoice. Judaism's message is one of happiness and delight in life. The rabbis of old said that the Divine Presence does not rest on man in the midst of sorrow or gloom. Do your best, recognize that being human you have frailties, overhaul your conscience at least once a year, and then rejoice with all the things which have been granted to you. For this rejoicing we have Succos.

But our joy must not take the form of complete abandon, and, as Jews, we may not celebrate by orgies, which were an integral part of the social and religious life of ancient peoples. Our rejoicing must be held within proper limits and we must avoid the excesses of joy as we must shun the extremes of sorrow. In whatever we do we must be guided by the textbook, the manual of life for the Jew, the Torah. It is that document whose principles have enabled us to survive. The concluding day of a unique holiday period is devoted to a reaffirmation of our loyalty to Torah which teaches us to be meditative without being depressed, and to be happy without becoming subhuman.

To me it seems that no season of the year is more appropriate for the celebration of a New Year than autumn. Whatever the historic reasons may be, I am concerned with the spirit and emotions of people at this period. In many ways there is a peculiar fitness which brings together Rosh Hashanah and autumn.

Spring is the season of promise, of youthful expectation, a harbinger of things yet to be. It does not bring with it a sense of memory; it speaks only of the future. One does not regret the passing of the chill blasts of winter. The buds of spring are only heralds of the beauty still to be unfolded.

Then comes summer, when everything is in full bloom. We cannot get enough of it and sigh with regret as each day passes. It is the time of vacation and we want to live only in the present. We desire to forget our jobs, our work, our responsibilities. We avoid thinking of what lies beyond the summer. We know only that it is good to be alive, and being alive in the summer is often synonymous with a desire to do nothing.

Think now of winter when the trees stand somberly covered with snow, like groups of old people who no longer have vitality, and are merely impressive relics of a grandeur that has passed. It is the season in which one lives in the past, a season whose rigors are softened by the recollection of joys already experienced.

But autumn is the most glorious of seasons. It subtly combines the past and present by a mysterious process. The leaves are still green without presenting that air of heaviness that hangs over summer. The wind stirs the blood in our veins and bids us move. It is the call to return to work, a reminder that life cannot be lived by doing nothing. Children return to school and we realize that vacation is over. It is time to harvest what has been planted and carefully tended, to see the reward of our labors. It isn't spring, to be sure, but it's also not yet winter. We combine the experience of the past with our joy of living. This is the season to be alive. And if one does nothing more than get outdoors, and walk or sit and converse with those we love, we shall feel the grandeur of living maturely and realize that the passage of time need not depress us, but can inspire us to understand the deeper values of existence.

In the religious calendar of the average Jew, the festival of Shevuot plays an insignificant part. Judging by synagogue attendance alone, the important holidays would seem to be Rosh Hashanah and Yom Kippur. Yet it is obvious to anyone who knows even the elementary facts about Judaism that if there were no Shevuot there would be no High Holy Days as they are often called.

Shevuot commemorates the great occasion when, to the Israelites at Mt. Sinai, the Torah was given. There may be varying opinions as to what actually happened in the wilderness of Sinai, but it is certain that an awe-inspiring event took place there, an event that fashioned the life of the Jewish people, an event that brought together God and man, heaven and earth. The Torah became the inheritance of the House of Jacob.

As the word is commonly used, Torah refers to the Five Books of Moses or to the parchment scroll on which they are written. But Torah means infinitely more than that. It designates the Law by which our people has lived, it describes a way of life, it involves a period of development and interpretation at the hands of the rabbis, it stands for the academies of Babylonia and Spain, North Africa and France, the yeshivot of Vilna and Wolozhin, the scholarly work of Zunz, Frankel, and Schechter.

But above all, Torah represents order and discipline. Beyond all the detailed provisions found in the Torah is the basic principle that human life must be subjected to law and that anarchy eventually leads to the destruction of everything man has laboriously created.

This is particularly relevant to us and the problems we face. Around us are the signs of a disregard of laws. The music that assails our ears through various media is a cacophony which has no rules. Art is not guided by any principles and much of our literature lacks direction and form. It may be said that creativity cannot be hampered by rules, but Shevuot teaches us that we can create only if there are some rules by which we work.

The Jew was convinced that he could live more completely because there were laws by which he directed his life's activities. There is a legend that when God offered the Torah to Israel at Sinai He said, "If you accept this Torah, it will be well with you. But if you do not, then I shall turn the world back to its original chaos." This seems to be the choice before us. It is the threat which is built into the universe. The choice before us is to live by a law which we acknowledge or see our world revert to its primordial formlessness. To accept the rule of law is to celebrate Shevuos.

The passage of time is of small significance unless it brings with it a maturing of the mind and a growing appreciation of the beauty of the world around us. If we live, we grow older, but we must ask ourselves whether we also become wiser. Is not this the message of the psalmist, "So teach us to number our days that we may acquire a heart of wisdom?"

The advent of Rosh Hashanah means, for us as Jews, that a new period of time begins. But it is a season marking, not only a calendar change, but also an occasion for examining our lives, for reflecting on the past and projecting ourselves into the future.

If there is one idea which Judaism emphasizes at this time, it is man's ability to determine his lot. While external circumstances may set limits to what he can do, yet within these limits man is free to make choices and decisions. For us, as Jews, there is no determined course our lives must take. For others, life is like a computer, which, having been programmed in a certain way, continues to repeat what was put into it in the past. The errors are constantly reproduced. Many people, having paid a bill recorded on a computer, continue to receive the statement of indebtedness many times because the machine is geared to repeat its past.

The religious lesson of Rosh Hashanah is that man has it within his power to improve or to hurt himself. The development of a taste for art, music, and literature, the refinement of the senses, the abolition of poverty, hatred, and war, the beneficient use of our environment, the elimination of misunderstandings on college campuses—all of these are in the hands of man.

Judaism does not believe in dropping out or turning off, forsaking the world because one thinks it irremediable, and finding refuge in a shadowy world which one enters by the use of drugs. The recognition of evil and ugliness in the world is our first duty, but it is coupled with an equal responsibility to help set things right.

We are taught to be optimistic; fundamentally, this does not mean a Pollyanna attitude toward life. It means only that we have faith in man and in man's potential for betterment. We do not believe that what has been laboriously built must be totally destroyed because we despair of human nature.

Rosh Hashanah denotes renewal. It means that we can reprogram our lives, that we need not repeat the errors of the past.

The most joyous of all the Jewish festivals is undoubtedly Succot. It is the occasion when the Jew gives thanks for the blessings which he has received from the hand of God. In ancient times the farmer in Palestine, seeing the harvest which the Lord's goodness and his own work had produced, sang a song of gratitude for his good fortune.

But there was an important aspect of this celebration which needs to be emphasized constantly. The Torah commanded the Jew to share his bounty with the poor, the widow, and the orphan. His joy could not be complete unless he shared what he had with another human being. The importance of this element remains constant down through the ages.

It seems that man was created incomplete by divine forethought so that part of his destiny on earth should be to achieve fulfillment through association with another human being. Love and marriage are the result of sharing, children give us the opportunity of sharing, our fellowmen make possible the exercise of sharing. This idea is exemplified in the opening formula of the Passover seder, "Let all who are hungry come and eat," and it is underlined on Succot when we are commanded to share our harvest with others.

Young children tend to be selfish, and part of attaining maturity consists of learning to share what is ours with others. The sense of possession is strong, yet life would be well-nigh impossible if we were unable to share with others those things we enjoy.

On the face of it, i.e., mathematically, it would seem that the more I share, the less I have for myself. But, in the realm of the spirit this is not true. It seems paradoxical, but it is true, nevertheless, that when we share our sorrows they become diminished, but when we share our joys they are increased.

Succot is the festival of thanksgiving and it must help us to answer an important question. Do we feel the need to share with others more when we feel the pinch of hunger, the pangs of sorrow, than when we enjoy the good things of life? Is it Yom Kippur or Succot which has the greater power to move us to share with our fellowmen? The 58th chapter of Isaiah which we read as the Haftarah on Yom Kippur admonishes us to share our possessions with the poor and the homeless, and a biblical command read on Succot requires us to do this in the hour of joy. The word "companion," according to its root meaning, is, one who shares our bread. He who drinks with others is a friend, an associate, a fellow celebrant, but he who drinks alone is a drunkard. The difference lies in sharing.

The month of September is one in which many people change their dwelling places. Moving vans are busy transporting household furniture from one place to another. But this is also the season of the Solemn Days when Jews celebrate the advent of a New Year. As I thought of these two ideas, movement of place and movement in time, it struck me that they have certain features in common.

When people live in an apartment or a house for a certain length of time, they are bound to accumulate a great number of possessions whose right to stay with them is not questioned. But when we prepare to move, and objects are dragged out from every nook, we stop to examine them with a critical eye. Shall we take these things with us or leave them behind? As a general principle, all of our household effects are put into one of three classes. First, there are the things that are absolutely necessary and that we must take with us. Secondly, there are objects which do not have a particular use but which we would not think of abandoning because they have sentimental value. They are bound up in memory with some member of the family or associated with some significant event. Finally, there are things we have accumulated over a period of time but now recognize as useless and which we leave behind us.

What is true of moving from place to place applies also to our movement in time. As we approach a new year we have the opportunity, denied us during the rest of the year, of looking over our mental and spiritual furniture. We surely will take with us our faith in God and in our fellowmen, our friendships and devotion to our tasks. These are things that we need. There are certain attitudes that we will take with us in the new year because they have sentimental value: the memory of certain events, a few words spoken to us under special circumstances, the clasp of a friendly hand, the word of encouragement or sympathy. These may have no practical value, but we will take them along. But there are also those things we should and must leave behind. If the spirit of the sacred days means anything to us, we must discard the petty jealousies, the baseless hatreds, the unfounded prejudices, the unholy greed, and the silly pursuits with which we have filled much of our days.

A new year is a moving day for the soul of the Jew, and every individual must look through his spiritual equipment in order that he may be adequately prepared for the days which lie ahead.

We are now celebrating one of the most important if not the most important of the Jewish festivals, Shevuot. And, if holidays can be so classified, it is likewise the humblest of all the festivals.

The Feast of Weeks (Shevuot) is not distinguished by any special rite, i.e., there is no sounding of a shofar, no building of a Succah, no eating of a particular diet, no kindling of special lights, no abstinence from food, and no planting of trees. Shevuot is a holiday which outwardly has no distinguishing mark. It is not specifically designated for observance on a certain day, as are all other Jewish festivals. The Bible, in describing the events surrounding the celebration of Shevuot, merely says that they occurred in the third month after the departure of the children of Israel from the land of Egypt. Tradition (not biblical prescription) has designated the celebration as falling on the sixth day of Sivan.

What took place on that day determines the total character of our religious belief, for it was the day of Revelation. No matter what interpretation we give to that event, all Jews must concede that something world-shattering and awe-inspiring occurred on Mt. Sinai on that day. Stated briefly, it may be said that there man confronted God; and the words spoken and taught at that time remain the imperishable treasure of the whole world. It is worthy of note that Mt. Sinai was the least majestic, least attractive of the mountains. It was chosen deliberately, say the rabbis, because of its lowly, humble character. And, as if to reinforce the lesson of humility, the man who stood on that humble mountain, acting as the liaison between God and his people, was Moses, of whom the Bible says that he was very humble, more so than any other human being.

This background of Shevuot, the humble festival, with its unattractive setting, and its humble hero, presents us with a most important lesson. We received the Torah at Sinai, but we have not made it part of our lives. Humility has not yet been learned; but on the contrary we strive to impress others with our importance and we assign value to insignificant things.

People attend services and are impressed with a Bar Mitzvah boy who has a pleasant voice and reads a Haftarah without a mistake. Yet it may well be that this efficient performer will drop any interest in things Jewish the day after his smooth performance. A rabbi is judged very often by his ability to devise gimmicks, to do what looks impressive in announcements but has no substance or lasting benefit behind it. People are judged frequently by their socially correct bowing and greeting, their observance of protocol, without any inquiry as to whether there is any warmth or sincerity behind the correct manners. Merchandise which is defective is attractively packaged and cleverly advertised and is sold on the basis of these questionable qualities. The honest, humble, unobtrusive ware or person goes unobserved and unappreciated in a world where salesmanship is more esteemed than sincerity.

If acceptance of Torah has any meaning for us, it must mean a restoration of the real, a return to sincerity, an appreciation of humility. It was a great Jewish prophet who taught us that God Himself dwells with those who are contrite and humble in spirit.

An interesting sight met my eyes as I was walking along one of the streets of our community. In the window of an apartment there was displayed a cut-out paper menorah indicating that this was the season of Hanukah. With all the Christmas wreaths which I had seen, this menorah seemed a bit lost, until I reflected that it was the symbol of our numerically small Jewish people which, through the ages, has endeavored to bring light to the world, to teach it the supremacy of the spirit over brute force.

It surprised me to learn subsequently that there were several individuals who felt that while it was right to kindle the lights of Hanukah in the home, it was not seemly to make a display of the festival publicly. After all, ran the argument, we are living in a non-Jewish country. It is well that Jews who feel this way should be enlightened.

According to the requirements of Jewish law, the place for Hanukah lights is where they can be seen by the passer-by, so that, in the words of the rabbis, "the miracle (of Hanukah) may be made public." Rightly understood, even the non-Jewish world should celebrate the Feast of Lights with us because it represents the first struggle for religious freedom. Had the Maccabees been defeated, the whole story of Western civilization might have been altered. It was not only the light in the Temple that was rekindled by Judah and his followers, but also the light that dispelled the darkness of idolatry and a decadent civilization.

Some of the people who object to a public display of the symbols of Hanukah do not hesitate to make a display of their financial status by arranging lavish social functions or spending money in a manner which draws attention to the least desirable elements in Jewish life. One cannot possibly overestimate the harm that is done by the ill will engendered by such displays. As a matter of fact, Jewish history records instances in the Middle Ages when the rabbis found it necessary to order Jews to refrain from an excessive display of wealth in order not to arouse the hostility of non-Jewish neighbors. There were strict regulations even as to the number of rings which Jewish women might wear and the materials of which their clothes might be made.

Let us understand one thing clearly. We have not and will not bring any harm to the fair name of the Jewish people by showing that we are observing the tenets of our faith or the historic festivals of our people. History has taught us that it is far more desirable to show what we are rather than what we have.

RELIGION

The writer of a recent article describing a certain clergyman says, in passing, "The minister is one of the last remaining members of our society who can't afford specialization." This statement is an apt description of the role of the modern rabbi as a "general practitioner," a role which many laymen do not sufficiently understand. Whereas the rabbi of earlier times concerned himself largely with scholarship, with a small measure of communal activity, the modern Jewish religious leader must give much of his time to helping people with their problems.

We rabbis must be "pediatricians." We are called upon to deal with children, with their educational and disciplinary problems, with the Bar and Bat Mitzvah. But this is only the beginning.

Into our offices come people who lack adequate vision or whose vision needs correction. Then we must act as spiritual ophthalmologists. This can become a very difficult task.

The tensions of modern life are many, and increasing numbers of people are coming to their rabbis, who, if they do nothing else, provide a listening ear and a sympathetic spirit for those who are troubled.

We must frequently fulfill the role of a cardiologist, i.e., deal with affairs of the heart. This means discussion and advice in situations involving men and women, intermarriage, and domestic misunderstandings.

In every community, there are people who find it difficult, if not impossible, to make their peace with the world. They complain about the harshness of life and we must convince them that the fault lies not so much in life as in the "liver."

What does one say to an unhappy person who, in his words, is "eating his heart out" over an unalterable situation? We must act, in such a case, as spiritual cardiologists and gastroenterologists. To adjust such an individual to life is by no means easy. To even attempt the task compels us to be amateur psychiatrists. And we find often that the person who thinks his problem is with respiration, actually is suffering from faulty aspirations.

The boundaries of our "practice" reach, increasingly, into the domain of geriatrics, and we must try to bring hope and a reason for living to people of advancing years.

Finally we must practice orthopedics, and endeavor to assist people who cannot stand on their own feet. To do this we must also be radiologists, having the ability to see through those who come to us.

The rabbinate, like the ministry of every religious denomination, is a complex profession with many branches. Ours is not a specialized calling. We try to be, and I hope we succeed in some measure in being, "generous practitioners."

More important than colored lights, decorated trees, greeting cards or Santa Clauses, is the religious message of this holiday season of our Christian neighbors. "Peace on earth, good will to men"—these words are sung, recited and engraved upon cards. This is the proclamation of Christmas.

But one is forced to admit that high-sounding as this statement is, it remains only a statement. Despite the sincere, but extremely vague pronouncements of the head of the church, there is no peace on earth and no good will among men. In the contemporary world, peace has come to mean a cease-fire, an armistice, a rest period between wars; and good will among men has proven to be either an ecumenical dialogue or a contribution to the fund for the neediest. We have not yet faced the fact that we must treat human beings as creatures made in God's image, as living beings who are valuable for themselves, and not because of the use we can make of them.

The Hebrew word for "peace" (shalom) is related to the word shalame, which means "whole." And it should remind us that there can be no peace among men unless we learn to look upon others in their completeness. What does this mean?

It means that I must realize that my fellowman is more than a competitor, in business, sports or in the classroom. It signifies that my fellowman is more than a Republican or Democrat, that he is infinitely more than my employee. It denotes that my fellowman is more than the representative of an ethnic group or of an economic class. It asks that I look upon my fellowman not as one whose religious outlook differs from mine or whose national origins are not the same as my own. It signifies that the moral lesson to be learned from the opening chapters of the Bible is that we being children of a common ancestor, every person is equal and valuable in the sight of God.

The people with whom we work and associate are, to be sure, our friends, competitors, co-religionists, fellow-citizens, civil servants, political opponents, but also human beings whom we should love and understand. The great danger to our interpersonal relationships arises from the fact that we fragmentize our fellowmen. The phrase "putting things together" has gained currency in our time. It is the totality of a human being which precedes every effort to achieve good will among men and peace on earth. Let those who, despite their pious protestations, harbor ill will and bitterness, think of this as they celebrate the birth of one whom they deem the savior of mankind. We need to celebrate the birth of a new kind of man more than we need to celebrate the birth of an alleged god.

Some events seem so improbable that we cannot bring ourselves to think of them. We are so accustomed to a certain way of life, that any sudden change seems unthinkable. And, then, without warning, activity is brought to a standstill. There is some mechanical difficulty in power transmission, and populous cities are plunged into darkness. The wheels of civilized living grind to a halt, and people are bewildered, lost, disorganized, and even terrified. What millions experienced during the past week is a very slight taste of what might happen if a warlike act were committed against us. This, if nothing else, should remind us of the horror of war and of the need for striving to advance the cause of peace.

While the exact cause of the blackout is, at this writing, unknown, it seems probable that the difficulty was in the transmission and not in the production of the electricity which supplies the light. This circumstance led me to think how much of the difficulty we encounter in dealing with children and young people can be attributed to our failure of transmission. The ideals are at hand, the principles are well known, but very often we fail to convey them to our children because the means we use are faulty.

There is one thing more which we may learn from the sudden darkness which overwhelmed about thirty million people, that is humility.

We have become greatly impressed with our achievements, with our ability to send men into outer space, to plumb the depths of the sea, to break the sound barrier with newly designed planes, to penetrate into the innermost secrets of nature. And yet a break in a power line which may be infinitesimal in size, can paralyze our bustling cities and deflate our pride in our achievements. It is at such a time that we realize how much our welfare and our ability to function depend upon, literally, a thread.

In all the years of my life, there have been bright, sunny days and cloudy days. Yet I cannot remember any day on which, after the night, the sun failed to appear. There was never a power failure in any part of the natural world. From this I can draw only one conclusion. The Cosmic Engineer is evidently more expert than the consultants of Con Edison.

When I was a boy, I recall that my companions and I, with a desire for sweets, used to buy chocolate made in the form of cigarettes. These were packaged in a box made in imitation of a cigarette brand. All of us could have chocolate and at the same time pretend that we were smoking, which was regarded as a sign of being grown up. Confectioners used their knowledge of the psychology of children in creating this form of candy.

With an understanding of unexpressed gastronomical desires of many Jews, there has now been created a new product. I saw it advertised in an Anglo-Jewish publication the mention of whose name might cause some embarrassment. I now know that McCormick and Company, Inc. (which calls itself "The House of Flavor") is producing a product called "Imitation Bacon Bits," under strict rabbinical supervision. Is this surprising? What is even more startling is that these Bacon Bits may even be used with dairy meals. "For a new taste thrill," (says the advertisement) "spread your Sunday bagel with cream cheese mixed with Imitation Bacon Bits K certified Kosher—Parve."

Let me make it very clear that I am not questioning the fact that the product is kosher and that it is made from "pure vegetable ingredients." But what troubles me is the idea that a food, under rabbinical supervision, must use the "bacon" designation to promote its sale. This is a very clear indication that an enterprising food manufacturer is capitalizing on what he sees as a subconscious desire of Jews to eat what is forbidden by Jewish Dietary Law.

This is not the only example of pandering to the tastes of those who want to "stay kosher" but want also the have the "thrill" of being a little bit a "goy." Dinners I have attended begin with a course of flaked fish, resembling (I am told) a crabmeat cocktail. It is kosher, of course, but one may ask why it must be made to resemble something else. The answer, I suppose, might be, that it's just for the "*halibut*."

The producers of the new "Bacon Bits" could enlarge the number of alluringly titled foods. I'd suggest Kosher Ham Knishes and Kosher Pork Kreplach, under rabbinical supervision. But of course, kosher-meat bacon strips are already on the market.

There are Jews who have a secret predilection for pork and a hankering for ham. McCormick and Company now gives them the chance to live "dangerously" in the domain of ritual. For me all these people are little boys who smoke chocolate cigarettes.

An expression that is frequently used suddenly acquired new meaning when I heard it recently. In describing some delicious food she had tasted, a woman said, "It was out of this world." This statement made me think that in the minds of many people, if a thing is to be perfect it cannot be of this world. The implication seems to be that conditions in the world in which we live make it impossible to attain the heights of joy or maximum satisfaction here. If one raises the objection that we must reluctantly content ourselves with the situation as it exists, we may answer that in the not too distant future, men may establish themselves on the moon. It will then be interesting to receive a message from lunar residents, telling us how it feels to be "out of this world." The subject is more than material for science fiction. It is bound up with man's entire outlook upon life which determines his conduct and happiness.

Frequently I am asked about the attitude of Judaism toward the question of life after death, about what happens after we leave this world. The correct answer is that in Judaism ideas about the hereafter are vague and general. We do not have an official description of what the future will be like, and even the references to the subject which we have, are undoubtedly the result of influences exerted upon us by other faiths. It may be that this disturbs many who look for assurance and certainty. As Jews, however, we feel that we cannot barter a working world for a problematic paradise.

Our people, down through the ages, has emphasized the need for leading a good life here, for creating the conditions that will establish a just and peaceful social order for helping bring to earth the kingdom of heaven. There was so much to be done in daily life as to leave little, if any, time for speculation concerning a future existence. For the Jew, it was enough to believe that what made him human and distinguished him from the beasts of the field, the divine element in him, would somehow survive his physical death.

The propulsion of human beings into space and their arrival upon the moon is a fascinating prospect. We will undoubtedly learn much in the future about the universe in which we live. But we must not adopt a concern for something outside of our own earth as being better than what we now possess. Our task is to rid this world of its evils, most of them man-made. "Out of this world" is for astronauts and physicists. "Of this world" is for the men and women who populate it.

72

At this season of the year, many statements are published and sermons delivered on the desirability of achieving peace. These sentiments are particularly significant this year which has witnessed the intensification of the Vietnamese struggle and the death of hundreds of Americans in the rice paddies and jungles of a long-suffering little country. Pope Paul has asked that the first day of the new calendar year be set aside as an occasion of prayers for peace. But at the same time he has rebuked those who may not agree with his method of achieving peace.

It is desirable to pray for peace. Certainly, no Jew needs to be reminded of this. Our constant greeting is "Shalom," our Amidah prayer ends with a plea for peace, and the priestly blessing concludes on a note of peace.

But it behooves us to recognize what is the nature of peace and what we must do to bring it into being.

Peace means more than the mere cessation of hostilities between individuals or nations. It means the recognition of the dignity of every human being and the respect which is due every nation, large or small. It means the right of men to develop their highest potentialities, to speak their minds, to protest against injustice and openly to oppose war. Two clergymen, speaking for the World Council of Churches, made it clear that "In the pursuit of peace, nations as well as churches must recognize that men of conscience differ as to the rightness of methods to be followed."

It is well to pray for peace but it is enlightening to read of the road to its attainment in the Psalms. We are told there that if we desire life, then "Desist from evil and do good, seek peace and pursue it." To abolish the evil and do what is right are steps which must be taken before peace can be achieved. Whether it is an individual or a group, whether it is peace within ourselves or directed outward, there can be no peace without love and the deeds of loving kindness. We must be prepared to pay as well as to pray for peace.

Two little boys, pupils in our school, were sitting on the stairs inside the building, writing something in their notebooks. Out of curiosity I stopped and asked them what they were doing. "We're doing our homework," said one of them. They were busily at work discussing the answers to questions which their teacher had given them, and making the identical grammatical mistakes. Similingly I asked, "It this the place to do homework? If it's done here, it's not what your teacher wanted."

"Well," answered one of the boys, "I didn't get a chance to do it at home so I do it here."

I suppose grown-ups will think this incident somewhat amusing, but it reflects an attitude which characterizes them as well as these little boys.

One of the great problems in Jewish education arises from the fact that too many Jewish parents want to do their "homework" in school. They fail to provide a proper atmosphere for their children in the home, they do not furnish their homes with even the semblance of a Jewish library, they show their youngsters no dignified observance of Jewish festivals. Parents have neglected the practice of daily worship in the home and they do not attend the synagogue. They expect us in the school to provide their children with a facility in reading Hebrew which we ourselves acquired only as a result of constant use of the prayer book. We learned to read fluently because we made use of the language. But now we are asked to do in the school that which should be done at home.

It is this failure to provide a religious atmosphere at home which accounts for the list of instructions issued recently by the Board of Superintendents to teachers in our public schools. These instructions are directed to showing how children can be inspired with the teachings of religion. Here again we have an instance of the shifting of a parental burden to the shoulders of school authorities, where it definitely does not belong.

In the Shema prayer which Jews recite morning and evening we read, "And thou shalt teach them (i.e., the words of the Torah) diligently unto thy children, and thou shalt speak of them when thou sittest in thy house and when thou walkest by the way. . . ." It is worthy of note that before we do anything else, we must first speak of Torah in the homes. If we want Judaism to survive, we must not be like the little boys. We must remember that the school is not the place to do our homework.

The problems which face Jewish young people on the college campus were the subject of discussion by Hillel directors at their recent convention. Many speakers pointed out what is obvious to anyone who knows student life today: that the militancy of the sixties, the impassioned oratory, the senseless vandalism, the invasion of offices have given way to a different, quieter, more contemplative mood. Some even see an indifference to political involvement by the young.

What has taken the place of the discarded attitude is an interest in mystical, intuitive religious sects, a search for personal salvation. There is a revival of old-time gospel meetings, of which the new "Jesus people" are the best example. This change represents not merely a rethinking of attitudes toward organized religion but a significant shift of emphasis of the world outlook of young people. It is most important for Jews because it represents a tendency which is contrary to a basic Jewish concept and which is being accepted by Jewish students.

Judaism has never believed that every individual must "do his thing." Hillel, in the first century of the Common Era, said that if one were not for himself who would be for him? But he was quick to add, "But if I am only for myself, what am I?" Personal salvation in its accepted theological sense was unknown to Jews, and the appeal to be "saved" fell upon deaf ears. We do not believe in original sin and hence we did not need to be saved from it. For us, the example of Moses has always served as a model. When God threatens to wipe out the children of Israel and simultaneously preserve Moses, the leader of his people declines and makes it plain that he prefers to perish with his flock.

Most petitionary prayers in the traditional siddur (prayer book) are formulated in the plural. The confession of sin which we recite on Yom Kippur is also in the plural ("We have sinned," etc.) because all of us together assume responsibility for the sins committed in the community.

Furthermore, we have always challenged and denied the belief that any person or alleged divine character could atone for the sin of anyone else. Each individual was charged with his own wrongdoing.

This new form of campus religion is fundamentally the satisfaction of the same needs which were taken care of by drugs. All drugs were chemotherapy for the individual's frustrations while gurus and evangelical meetings are "theotherapy" for the same ailment. No longer concerned about the welfare of society and apathetic toward political involvement, young people now seek their own personal salvation. Those who profess to wait for the Second Coming of the Messiah will do nothing to bring about a better world. Dean Napier, a professor of religion at Stanford University, has said, "The Jesus movement is not going to lift a finger to change the status quo." As Jews, we cannot accept this. We must be involved in the world around us, in bettering the lives of our fellowmen. My own existence has meaning only if it is entwined with the lives of other human beings.

The subject of religion has concerned me for a long time, and, in the language of our day, I might say that I have a "hang-up" on the subject. But I find that I am being constantly challenged, as a religious person, to examine my beliefs and, perhaps, to revise certain opinions I have held.

Two recent events give me cause to ponder the question of the essence of religion and to face some basic problems.

A young man who applied for the honor of becoming an Eagle Scout (the highest rank in the Boy Scout movement) was denied (but later granted) the honor because his parents are atheists and he does not believe in God. There was nothing in his record to show that he was unethical or did not live in accord with the ideals of scouting except that he didn't believe in God.

However, there was a more serious situation of a similar kind in New Jersey, where a judge denied the right to adopt a child to a couple who have had her for sixteen of the seventeen months of her life, because they do not believe in God. The man and his wife have been found to be "persons of high ethical and moral standards." Both the judge and the adoption agency concur in this opinion; but where the agency favors the application, the judge does not. He feels that the child's eventual decision between belief and nonbelief should not be prejudiced by nonbelieving prospective parents.

It is time that honest people opened their eyes and divested themselves of much of the hypocrisy and pious mouthings of religious affirmations.

What does belief in God mean? German soldiers going out to show themselves the Master race, wore belts with buckles bearing the words "Gott mit uns" (God is with us). The administrators of the Inquisition in Spain tortured Jews on the rack for the sake of God. Klansmen in white sheets spoke in the name of a God who had created white people to be superior to other ethnic groups.

77

Countless martyrs have been burned at the stake for not believing in the "right" kind of God, and there is incessant agitation for bringing prayer into public schools so that children may affirm a belief in God.

I am a believer, but does that demand that I look down upon those who intellectually or emotionally do not accept religious belief? Is one less a decent human being if, living an upright life, he is an agnostic or an atheist? If I believe that the purpose of affirming a belief in God is to refine the human spirit, to make people upright, considerate, sympathetic, helpful, and magnanimous, shall I read out of my life those who achieve all these qualities on a nondeistic basis?

It is about time that we stripped away the insincerity, the hollowness which alas! have become attached to words like "love," "brotherhood," "patriotism," and, above all, "God." To face ourselves and to purge ourselves of the dross of artificial religiosity—this in itself is a manifestation of a belief in God.

What is faith? As the word is generally understood, it means acknowledgement of the existence of a Supreme Being and the reality of a divine order in the world. It means a religious system or a religious group to which one belongs. But faith means more than this. It conveys the idea of the certainty of goodness. To have faith in some person or thing means to be sure of his or its goodness. It means to accept as true that which cannot be demonstrated by rational proof or tangible evidence.

What is faith? It is the ability to say in the hour of sorrow that life is good, and that pain and bereavement are a natural part thereof. It is a rendering of thanks for the blessings we have enjoyed rather than a vain yearning after those we might have had.

What is faith? It is the recognition that the quality of a life is infinitely more important than its number of years. It is the memory of precious moments stored up in the heart, unforgettable experiences which punctuate the ordinary prose of life and give it meaning.

What is faith? It is the determination to make ideals live long after the one who professed them is no longer in existence. It is the ability to find solace in the association of the afflicted.

What is faith? It is the ability to feel the touch of a hand made cold by death, to hear across the great barrier the gentle, soothing voice of those we loved. It is the ability to face the trials of life with courage and to confront its problems with undimmed eye.

This is the meaning of faith.

One of the major developments in the religious thinking of our time is to be found in the idea of ecumenism, an attempt to bring men of different faiths closer to one another. The goal is to be reached not by watering down the principles of any religious group nor by arranging social functions at which one may compliment the other. An effort is to be made to re-think some fundamental Christian concepts, to examine historically the genesis of certain attitudes and to be prepared to relinquish entirely or to update ideas which have been cherished for a long time.

The road is a long one but there are some unmistakable signs of progress. What are they?

First, as a result of careful study, the story of the crucifixion is being retold in a different way. Among enlightened Roman Catholic and Protestant clergymen, Jews are no longer accused of deicide, and no longer is the accusatory finger being pointed at us because we allegedly killed a god. The Passion Play at Oberammergau still repeats this canard, but intelligent Christians do not repeat the charge.

Secondly, there has come a recognition of the significance of the State of Israel for the Jewish people. The overwhelming majority of Christians did not understand to what extent the land of Israel was important to the religious development of the Jewish religion. But now it is becoming clear to Christians that it is not a chauvinism or imperialism which underlies our devotion to the land, but rather a loyalty to Judaism which demands it.

Thirdly, Judaism is no longer regarded as the embryo whose only purpose was to develop into Christianity. For too long have Christians been taught that Judaism was merely a step on the road which led to the height of the Christian faith. Judaism has been recognized as an equal partner.

This new look at Judaism comes, in part, from a more intensive study of the Bible, the so-called Old Testament. Modern Christian scholars no long contort or misinterpret passages from the prophets to prove that they predicted the coming of Christianity's founder.

But just as significant as the change in theological thinking is the fact that, especially in the Roman Catholic church, the service begins to come closer to its Jewish origins. The attempt is being made for greater lay participation, and readings from the Bible are increasing. Even in communion, liberal Catholics want the use of more substantial food than the very thin wafer traditionally placed on the tongue of the communicant.

Groups within the Church want to make communion a more faithful reflection of the idea that it originated with the Passover Seder, and there are already some who advocate the use of matzos instead of the wafer.

We've come a long way. Perhaps one may look forward to the day when matzos, baked under rabbinical supervision, will be used at communion. That would truly symbolize a festival of redemption.

Every Friday, *The New York Times* carries announcements of synagogue services, which I always read with interest. I am sure that there is no malice on the part of the editor, but I feel somewhat disturbed by the fact that the synagogue notices are always on the page devoted to obituaries. Is that where the Sabbath service announcements belong? It seems strange to read of death in one column and to see sermon subjects like "The Deathlessness of Judaism" or "The Eternal Verities of Judaism" in another column.

I have wondered where the synagogue notices could appropriately be placed. There are many possibilities.

They might be placed on the sports page, because for many Jews, the synagogue is merely another social club. They do not attend services or classes, but look upon the religious edifice as an institution which satisfies their desire to be together with other people who are descended from a common ancestor, Abraham.

Perhaps synagogue notices should appropriately be placed on the financial page, because many Jews are concerned exclusively with the budget and fund-raising of the synagogue and not at all concerned with those values for which the money is being raised.

One might argue, with some justification, that the announcement of Sabbath services belongs on the theatrical or amusement page. The Friday-night service must often compete with popular TV shows, and the Saturday-morning service is often poorly attended because there are other attractions outside. Even in the synagogue, efforts are made to "put on a good show," to use the devices of showmanship to entice the worshipper.

The juxtaposition of synagogue notices and death notices has its virtues. It serves to remind us that in the hour of death, most people turn to religion. It is there where they expect to find consolation, it is to the religious leader that people turn with their unanswerable questions about human destiny. How and when death happened people know, but they ask, "Why?"

Perhaps the proper place for synagogue notices is on the "Help Wanted" page. It might indicate that what we Jews are saying is, "We need men and women who will come to the synagogue to worship, who are seriously concerned with preserving the spiritual heritage of the Jewish people, who feel no need for special effects in the service, who regard the synagogue as more than a social club." The synagogue is more than an adjunct to the funeral chapel. It is an agency which is looking for help.

A recent Gallup poll endeavored to ascertain the church-going habits of people in the United States. The results reveal that there has been a continued downward trend in attendance at public religious services in the last thirteen years. During 1971, only 40 percent of adults, on the average, attended synagogues or churches regularly. Roman Catholics show a drop from 71 percent in 1964 to 57 percent in 1971. For Jews, the figure is fairly constant at 19 percent.

On the face of it, these results would seem to be a cause for despair in the Jewish community, but this is not necessarily so. Too many people fail to distinguish between the role of the church and that of the synagogue.

For a Christian, church attendance is an indispensable element in living a Christian life. For the Protestant, the church is the place for worship, while for the Catholic it is the only place where mass can be celebrated. For all Christians, there are very few religious ceremonies and rites in the home. Perhaps a prayer before a meal or an occasional prayer may be recited. Hence the church occupies a very important place.

For a Jew, the situation is totally different. While we recognize the value of prayer and understand the value of worshipping with a congregation, yet we also are aware of the fact that the majority of Jewish religious observances are centered in the home. Dietary laws, the lighting of candles on the eve of the Sabbath and festivals, the affixing of a mezuzah to the door, grace after meals, the building of a succah, the purchase of a lulav and esrog—all of these and many more are involved in the life of an observant Jew at home. And even for prayer, any humble home can become as sacred as the most impressive synagogue. In brief, Judaism does not rise or fall by synagogue attendance.

Does this imply that public worship is unnecessary for Jews? Not at all. There is value in the association of Jews with one another which the synagogue provides. It engenders a spirit of identity with one's people and enables us to share the joys of others (even strangers to us) and to participate in their sorrows.

The traditional Jewish Sabbath service is not a brief one and this may be one reason why people do not attend the synagogue. Some may not be able to follow the service because of their limited knowledge of Hebrew; others may find the prayers irrelevant to their needs. Still others may object to institutionalizing prayer and may look upon a permanent, unchanging book of devotions as an outmoded piece of literature. One must not overlook the fact that for Jews, as for others, there is a growing number of diversions to take one away from the house of worship. I am sure that Hasidim in Polish and Russian towns were not tempted by a golf game on the Sabbath, nor was Tevyeh lured by ice-skating on that day.

All of the foregoing may help to make clear certain attitudes of Jews which may seem at first glance to be incomprehensible. We are not concerned about prayer in the public schools because our children are expected to pray at home and to render thanks to God for everything we enjoy. We did not originate the idea of an invocation before every public meeting because at practically every assemblage a word of Torah was bound to be spoken and for us the study of Torah was in itself a means of worshipping God.

Polls on synagogue attendance are not barometers of the strength of Jewish life. Nevertheless I'd like to ask, "Were you in *shul* last Shabbos?"

It is disturbing to find a growing tendency on the part of Jews to resort to clericalism. Let me explain that by clericalism I mean the faith of people that it lies within the power of the religious leader to bring about any desired result.

Through the ages, Jews have believed that everyone, rich or poor, learned or ignorant, exalted or lowly, stood as equals before God. The prayers of the humblest individual were regarded as equal to those of the greatest rabbi. There were no special powers vested in the religious leader by which he could do what an ordinary mortal could not.

But in Jewish life we have taken a page from the volume of political science. We have learned what is meant by the delegation of power. It is historically demonstrable, I think, that as religious knowledge and Jewish observance decreased, it was accompanied by an increased resort to and dependence on the rabbi to carry the burden of Jewish commitment and responsibility.

Lest all of this sound vague, let us make the matter more specific.

A Jewish boy is born. For reasons of their own, the parents have the child circumcised by a physician, often non-Jewish. They feel, somehow, that something is lacking—the religious element. In traditional fashion, a male child is named at his *bris*. Since there has been here no *bris*, but merely a surgical procedure, the parents want the rabbi to say a few words in the synagogue to name the child and to make up for their failure to follow Jewish law. Neither the rabbi nor any other person possesses such power or authority.

A similar situation arises in connection with mixed marriages. The bride, the groom, or the parents on either side feel that if they can persuade a rabbi to marry the couple, without a conversion on the part of the non-Jewish partner, the marriage will be "kosher." Sometimes it is even suggested that the rabbi participate together with a Christian clergyman. Let it be understood that the failure of a rabbi to comply with such requests has nothing to do with his attitude toward mixed marriage. It is only that rabbis have no power to change situations involving violation of Jewish law by saying some special words.

One more illustration comes to mind and it concerns perhaps a majority of Jews who still come to the synagogue, even if infrequently. I refer to the misconception concerning the rabbi's role in the celebration of a Bar Mitzvah. Why can't parents understand that the public appearance of a boy, on the Sabbath near his thirteenth birthday, and the reading of the Haftorah (prophetic portion) are not the important parts of what the name of the event itself indicates. "Bar Mitzvah" means one who is subject to the commandments. It is Torah study and religious observance that are essential. By all means, let us bring the boy to the synagogue and let us celebrate, but let us not confuse the essentials with the lesser aspects. The rabbi does not have the power to confer "Bar Mitzvah" on a boy, who becomes a Bar Mitzvah without anyone's intervention. No special ceremony is needed to confer adulthood on an adolescent.

If Jews would stop treating rabbis like clergymen and would realize that Judaism is a do-it-yourself religion, we would have a healthier climate in the Jewish community and there would be less reason for young people to question the sincerity of their elders.

A recent Gallup poll should be of interest to all Americans and especially to those who are religious-minded. More than 12,000 adults in several nations were interviewed in the poll and the results have now been made public. The questions asked were, "Which of the following do you believe in: Life after death? The devil? Hell? God?" We learn from the poll that Americans stand at the head of the list in affirmative answers to the questions, and Frenchmen are near the bottom of the list, running close to Swedes in their nonbelief.

While the statistics may be interesting, it seems to me that they do not tell us much about human beings except to give expression to their speculative processes. It is, I think, very important to ask some additional questions.

When, for instance, we learn that 98 percent of Americans assert a belief in God, we must inquire how it affects their lives. Only 73 percent of the French who were interviewed and only 60 percent of the Swedes affirmed such a belief. Are we Americans more ethical than these nationals? Is there more concern for human beings here than there is in either France or Sweden? Is our crime rate lower, are our international attitudes and relations any more altruistic than those of lesser-believing nations? In other words, what does belief in God do for us; how does it change our lives? If it is merely an affirmation of some conclusion as to the plan of the Universe, it is of little value. To put it in modern terms, belief in God is functional.

Similar considerations apply to a belief in the other matters about which inquiry was made. If one believes in the devil, does this mean that one recognizes the tendency of men to be selfish, arrogant, dishonest, and inconsiderate? Do the Gallup tabulations mean that Americans fight the devil within themselves and in society with more determination than others lower on the list?

If one believes in Hell, does he believe that it is a region inhabited by souls which have left the body, or does one think that it is possible to create a Hell here on earth? If one is convinced of life after death, does he believe that this is the lot of all or is it reserved for certain chosen ones? Does a belief in life after death create an accompanying conviction that somewhere, sometime, somehow we will be given an opportunity to make good some of our mistakes in the life we lead here on earth?

To me it seems that the value of a religious faith lies in what it does for man and for society here on earth. My knowledge of what is going on in the contemporary world does not convince me that the French and the Swedes are less noble human beings because percentage wise they are not as "religious" as Americans.

To feel as I do is to be in the mainstream of the Jewish attitude toward life and the world. Judaism was and is not essentially a speculative philosophy nor a mystic brooding. Rabbinic literature stresses the idea of the *mitzvah*, the deed which is inspired by a belief in God. It was clear to the sages of Israel that by the manner in which we act we reveal our beliefs. Only through our concern for others, through love and kindness, through unselfishness and mutual aid, can we make clear what are our fundamental convictions. Those who truly believe in God and in the worthwhileness of life, by their daily conduct, give evidence of the divine image within them.

The current issue of the *Reconstructionist* magazine contains an article by one of my colleagues who declares, "The sermon is dead." He sees no useful purpose to be served by preaching, and strikes out against the rabbis who seem to him to be assuming a posture of superiority over their listeners. What concerns me is not his Agnew-like use of alliteration or his attempt to impress the reader with the size of his prestigious congregation. I am disturbed at the attempt of my colleague to be au courant with the anti-Establishment people, to pander to the taste of those who desire to reduce all men to a common level.

In place of the sermon, my Western colleague wants to substitute "teaching." He describes how he placed several microphones in his synagogue and after initiating a discussion, he asked for comments and questions from the audience. All of this was done in the course of a religious service.

The very distinction which is drawn between preaching and teaching is offensive to me. It seems to my prejudiced mind that the sermon is, and should be, a lesson. It should shed light upon a biblical text or illumine a contemporary problem in the light of our rabbinic heritage. To criticize all sermons on the ground that they are irrelevant or oratorical displays of the half-baked sociological, political, or psychological notions of the rabbi, is an affront to my colleagues in the rabbinate. I fail to see how enlightening it would be for the worshippers to listen to some illiterate, exhibitionist people take the microphone (as they invariably do) and voice their inanities publicly.

The writer of the "sermon obituary" feels that the rabbi should come down from his eminence, dais, or pulpit and thus remove the difference between him and the congregant. This same demand has been voiced by all the anti-Establishment devotees. The leveling process represented by this attitude is, as I see it, one of the major threats to our way of life.

One of the marks of a civilized, cultured individual is his ability to make distinctions. We usher out the Sabbath with a prayer called *Havdalah* (separation). The word is used over and over again in Jewish life. We divide "between the sacred and the secular, between light and darkness, between the week-days and the Sabbath, between Israel and the nations of the world."

Unfortunately, our assembly-line, mass-production civilization has tended to eliminate all differences. Everything is reduced to a monotonous sameness, and quality is forgotten. A father becomes a pal to his son, a teacher is called by his first name by students, the dais or pulpit is eliminated and the rabbi comes down to the people, and there are even attempts to reduce the two sexes to one. In the synagogue this amounts to a social transvestism.

The rabbis of the Talmud say, *"Im ain deah, havdalah minayin?"* ("If there is no understanding, how can one expect a sense of discrimination?"). The reverse is likewise true. If the democratic process is to mean the elimination of all distinctions and the reduction of all intellectual efforts to the least common denominator, then we will have the rule of the mob.

When a Jew is called to the Torah, he is, in traditional terms, getting an *aliyah* (literally, "ascent"). This is an honor and it is eagerly sought by Jews in the synagogue. If the pulpit is eliminated, there is no chance for an *aliyah*. I do not mean to imply that the physical act of ascent is important but rather that we must recognize levels of attainment in life.

To my mind there is a difference between parent and child, teacher and student, rabbi and congregant. I am still enough of a snob to insist that there must be some distance between different groups. I am still establishment-minded enough to believe that there should be a congregation and also a pulpit with a rabbi on it. I believe that the rabbi should give his worshippers an "aliyah," i.e., bring them up to the pulpit rather than descend from it to their level.

One of the effects which Rosh Hashanah has upon the mind of the Jew is the acute awareness of the passing of time. We look back and comment upon how quickly the old year has sped as we contemplate, with some concern, the year which lies ahead. In our prayers we ask to be inscribed in the Lord's book for a good life. If I were asked to put into words what I mean by a good life, I would pray in this fashion:

Lord of the Universe, who has sustained me in life to this moment, I humbly present my petition to you. Preserve, in health, those who are dear to me, and enable me to do my duty to them. Let my eyes never be blind to the beauty of the world; let me feast my gaze upon the budding trees and flowers and let my spirit find delight as I see green leaves donning the multi-colored vestments of the fall season. Teach me to be patient and understanding in my dealings with my fellowmen. Enlighten me so that I may comprehend the suffering of others and help to alleviate their pain and raise them up when they stumble. Give me the ability to coax a smile to the face of the disheartened and to dry the tears of the bereaved. Attune my ear to the laughter and the prattle of little children so that I may through them renew my youth. Enable me to understand that the shortcomings I see in others may, unobserved, exist in me. As I want others to forgive me, so may I learn to forgive others and bear them no grudge. May my hand be used to greet my fellowman, to confer a blessing upon him and never to grasp the tools of war or to strike another human being. Endow me with the strength to fight bravely against the evils of ignorance, poverty, and war. Grant me the power to face myself frankly, to cut through the superficialities of life, the conventional insincerities, and to reach the essential core of honest feeling. May I never succumb to the blandishments of material success, and may I ever cherish the things which serve to enlarge and deepen my existence as a creature of your fashioning. Help me always to find meaning in my life and purpose in the pursuit of my daily tasks. Keep strong within me my attachment to my people, and may I be able to help in the preservation of the priceless spiritual achievements which make the Jewish people great. Strengthen within me the resolve to pursue my work and let me feel to the end of life that my task is left unfinished. May my prayers be joined with those who supplicate you for a world at peace. And when my end comes, O God, let me leave behind some achievement in behalf of my fellowmen which will serve as a token of my appreciation and gratitude for having been allowed to live here on earth.

This is my prayer for the New Year. May it bring health, happiness, and peace to us and to all mankind.

What does it mean to be a religious person? Does it mean only to practice certain rites and ceremonies? Does it signify only adherence to a creed and acceptance of certain theological concepts? Does it not involve a relationship to people which will prove our love for creatures made in the image of a God whom we worship? From some things which I have been reading, it would seem that the gap between religion and life is widening, with the result that organized religion exists as an enclave in our society. The ritual part of Jewish law is called *Orach Hayim* (the "Way of Life"), and unless religion is just that, it will be of no value to our contemporaries.

In a recent study made by two sociologists of the University of California, it was revealed that despite high-sounding, well-worded declarations, most American church members are racially and religiously prejudiced and, what is more, nearly one-third of the clergy is of the same mind. To make the situation an even more depressing one, is the finding of the sociologists that church members are more prone to prejudice than those who do not belong to the church. One might, on the basis of these results, arrive at a definition of religion as a God-centered, emotionally fortified underpinning for irrational hatred. It is not surprising to learn that the study reveals that a majority of church members are opposed to participation by their churches and clergy in the cause of civil rights. This is to be expected from people who do not want their religion to interfere with their lives. *The New York Times* quotes the report as saying, "One is almost forced to wonder if Christians are afraid to have Negroes as neighbors for fear that then they would have to love them."

Another study on prejudice in the schools says, "Prejudice is a white gentile problem." To me, as a Jew, it is somewhat conforting to know that it is not a Jewish problem. Never, in the long history of our people, have we preached or taught our children to hate people of different religious convictions from our own or to despise them because of their color. But, honesty compels us to admit that there are Jews who forget what Judaism teaches and engage in acts which negate our teachings of love and understanding.

There is nothing more damaging to the cause of religion than the failure of its professed adherents to live up to its teachings. The easiest kind of religion is that which is professed; the hardest kind is that which is lived. Prejudice is a denial of religion, just as understanding is its affirmation.

A birthday should be more than a numeral on a calendar. It should awaken certain thoughts within us and be utilized as an opportunity for examining our lives.

For a child, a birthday is the synonym for a party and gifts. If it is the thirteenth birthday and the person is a boy, it means the ceremony of Bar Mitzvah (if a girl, Bat Mitzvah) and all the festivity which generally accompanies it. When we are very young we want to hurry the birthdays and grow up fast. When we are older we regard birthdays as grim reminders of the swift passing of time and of the decreasing supply of years left to us.

Perhaps the best wish one can make on his birthday is to repeat the utterance of the psalmist, "So teach us to number our days that we may acquire a heart of wisdom." What is important is the recognition that as we become a year older we should, at the same time, be a year wiser. Do we understand ourselves better than we did a year ago? Has the lapse of one year changed our outlook on life to any extent? Do we appreciate the fact that as we grow older, our habits and activities must be adjusted to the physical and psychological changes which take place within us?

There are people who deem it a great compliment to be told that they "haven't changed a day in the last twenty years." To me, it seems a sad reflection that one hasn't changed over a period of years. The urge always to stay young is an affliction of the spirit which is contrary to the intent of nature. It was intended that we should grow more mature with the years, that the experiences of life should provide us with a wisdom which only the years can bring.

It is noteworthy that the psalmist asks, not for wisdom in the ordinary sense of the term, for mental acumen, for increased comprehension of facts; he asks for "a heart of wisdom." What does this mean? It signifies a heart that understands the suffering of others, a heart that responds to the call for aid, a heart that beats in unison with that of a friend, a heart that can discern sincerity, a heart that can speak although no words are uttered. Thus, as we count another year in our lives, our prayer should be for "a new heart and a new spirit," a supplication for increased knowledge and sympathy, mellowness, and love.

It is frightening—there are children all around—big ones and little ones—boys and girls—two ladies who are the teachers —chairs, games, wooden blocks—a smock for each child—all kinds of pictures on the walls and words which one cannot yet read—this is school: it is the first day. And mothers remain for a short while in sight of their children and then they go to another room, there to wait until the pupil is accustomed to play with others without the presence of his mother.

Who can fathom the depths of the emotions of a child who trembles in fear that he is being forsaken? The little boy or girl who cries is even less of a problem than the one who puts on a bold front but is terrified beyond measure.

What does the new pupil fear? The answer is, being alone, not having a hand to hold, not having some loving one to soothe you if you should hurt yourself. To feel alone and to look upon oneself as a stranger in his surroundings is a devastating experience.

At this season of the year, all of us become contemplative. We think of the blessings and the troubles of a year which is ending and, standing on the threshold of a new year, we peer anxiously into the future. What the New Year may bring us is, of course, shrouded in uncertainty. But one concern is embedded deeply within us, viz., that we should not feel alone, that we should not see ourselves as abandoned. I say "feel" alone and not "be" alone because it is possible to feel alone in the midst of many people, like the first-day pupil in the classroom.

If Judaism—or, for that matter, any religion—has a contribution to make to human well-being, it is to be found in its efficacy in overcoming the sense of loneliness. To be a religious person means to face life with the conviction that there is some power in the universe which accompanies, assures, and strengthens us. It is expressed in the words of the psalmist, "Although I walk (alone) in the valley, I will fear no evil, for You are with me." In the words of the title of a profound religious work (by Prof. Abraham Heschel), "Man is Not Alone."

But to be fully happy we need not only have the assurance of a cosmic companion, but also the feeling that there is at least one human being whose hand we can touch, and to whom we can turn for emotional support. It is this thought that gives us the ability to go on despite obstacles, disappointments, and defeats.

We greet people by taking their hands and thus exchanging, without words, our feelings for one another. It is good to know that in a confusing, often hectic, daily existence, we have not been abandoned, that somewhere in the background there is a dear friend, that we are not alone.

A considerable number of Roman Catholics, in this country and elsewhere are opposing the recital of the mass in the vernacular despite permission to do so from the Vatican, and are insisting on retaining the original Latin text. On the face of it, this may seem like the attitude of die-hards who resist all innovation and progress, but I can understand and also sympathize, to a large extent, with these "conservatives."

Language is not merely a vehicle for stating facts or expressing ideas. It is also a medium for giving utterance to our emotions. Almost unconsciously we invest our words with an emotional content so that certain words evoke definite feelings. A person steals money which is entrusted to him. To say "steal" might make a common thief of the individual, so we say he "misappropriated" the funds. It is discovered that someone is afflicted with a serious disease called "cancer," but no one uses the word, except, perhaps, the physician. People will generally describe the affliction as a "malignancy" because that word is emotionally less disturbing. If we talk about an unattractive woman, we don't say she is not pretty, but we speak of her as "plain." And when someone's life is over, we do not use the word "died," but say rather that he "passed away."

All these examples serve merely to show that we avoid using certain words and use others that mean the same thing, because those we use are less disturbing to us emotionally.

It is understandable that those who attend religious services should want to know the meaning of the words they utter. It seems an exercise in futility to mouth sentences whose significance is lost on the worshipper. Every effort should be made to let the individual know in what he is participating. But there still remains an area where words, even if not understood, convey a profound meaning. There are also words whose meaning we feel, whose sense we understand, but which we cannot translate into any other language.

Does *mitzvah* mean a "meritorious deed?" It does, but it means much more. What does *chutzpah* signify? Is it synonymous with "boldness?" It is, but it also signifies a special kind of boldness.

If we were to eliminate Hebrew from the service, would the declaration, "Hear, Oh Israel" be nearly as significant as "Shema, Yisroel?" Would a mourner who does not understand Hebrew but whose heart is touched by the loss of a loved one, be moved as much by saying, "Magnified, and sanctified be His great name," as by reciting, "Yisgadal v'yiskadesh Sh'mei Rabbah?"

The Roman Catholic who wants to hear the mass in Latin, no less than the Jew who prays in Hebrew, feels the power of words, hallowed by tradition, which arouse within him feelings independent of the meaning of those words. The proclamation of God's unity *(Shema)* and resignation to His will *(Kaddish)* are deeply felt even if not intellectually understood.

Valuables are things which have meaning for us, and it is understandable that we should bestow care upon them and protect them from harm. People are advised to put their valuables in a vault and many do so. What is generally placed there? Insurance policies, bonds, stock certificates, deeds to property, cash, and jewelry. These are the things which we call "valuables."

Yet, even a moment's thought should convince us that what is most precious in life cannot be put into a vault. The smile on the lips of a child, a warm handclasp, a sympathetic tear, the sound of music—these cannot be shut within the confines of a steel vault, yet who will deny that they are "valuables?"

But what amused and startled me simultaneously was a radio announcement that a warehouse company has constructed vaults in the mountains to protect valuables against the destruction of a nuclear weapon attack. The bombs may fall and wipe out every vestige of civilization, millions of people may die and those who survive may find life worse than death, but we can be consoled with the thought that our "valuables" will be safe. Have we reached a stage in the world's history when an old rabbinical legend is enacted before our eyes?

In connection with the building of the Tower of Babel described in the Bible, the rabbis of the Midrash say that when a brick slipped from the hands of a mason, there was a lament, but that when a human being lost his foothold and plunged to his death, no one expressed any regret. Bricks were more important than people.

It is often discouraging to see the great care which is bestowed on material possessions when contrasted with an indifferent attitude toward the welfare of human beings. One person, no matter how humble his station in life, is more precious than all the accumulated wealth of the world.

The plot of a short story is developing in my mind. It is several weeks after an atomic attack on our country. As far as the eye can see there is debris. Workers are digging in the ruins and they discover a steel box near the foot of a mountain where a warehouse company had placed it. They open the box and find in it several hundred shares of stock in a company which manufactures missiles.

THE PERSONAL LIFE

The desire to get ahead and to succeed in life is understandable and praiseworthy, but it must be watched very carefully lest it deteriorate and become an overpowering drive which can ruin the highest ideals of life. In intimate relationship with the desire for success stands the love of honor. That we should crave recognition is perfectly natural, but that this craving should be satisfied at the cost of riding roughshod over others is both irreligious and inhuman.

If one becomes interested in a cause, we have a right to assume that he is convinced that it is worth while Beyond the satisfaction of knowing that one is helping achieve some great objective, there should be no expectation of any other reward. If honors come, they should be regarded as a bonus which one is glad to receive but cannot claim as a right.

It is pathetic to see how often people are offended because their names are not mentioned at a public function or because their names are unintentionally omitted from a program. The fact that their feelings are wounded by such petty things could be overlooked and forgiven if these people did not make the state of their feelings so obvious. One observes them and is impelled to laugh at their strategy in calling attention to themselves.

Poor, unhappy men and women who are not content until they are sure you know whose hand they have shaken and which celebrity they can call by a first name. And, if you don't know these facts, they do not hesitate to tell you about them. The important thing is that you must be impressed. These seekers after honor do not realize that they betray their pitiable insecurity and feelings of inferiority by their attitude. They do not understand the words spoken by Emerson, "I cannot hear what you say because what you are speaks so loudly."

When one gazes upon a beautiful stage set, he is impressed by the ingenuity involved in fashioning the sight before our eyes. But if we were to walk behind this scenery and see the struts and the props, the rags and the paint—the materials of which it is made—I am sure that much of our delight in it would vanish. Similarly, the sight of a person playing an active role in communal affairs is a sight which makes us rejoice. However, as soon as we discover the mechanism that impels people to work, our enthusiasm wanes. Wisely did the rabbis of old say that honor eludes him who chases after it, for, if one pursues it, it ceases to be an honor.

From the lips of an intelligent young man, I heard the statement, "I, and many like me are unhappy, because we have been disillusioned. Life for us is the supreme disappointment. We start out in life with bright hopes that are never realized. We come to understand that we were silly to have cherished any dreams."

The subject of my conversation with this unhappy young man is entirely too profound for any brief examination and too vexing for an immediate answer. But I feel that even a brief rejoinder may serve some useful purpose.

We must start out by distinguishing between delusion and illusion. We begin life with delusion. Our senses deceive us with respect to distance, shape, and color. The earth moves, the sun stands still; what seems elliptical turns out to be circular. All of our experience turns out to be a correction of life's delusions, and we must realize that the disappointment is merely the mistake of our conceptions. This is delusion.

If we paint wood so that it looks like marble, this is delusion. But if we paint a picture of trees and sky which are not mistaken for what they seem, yet produce an emotion through the picture which real trees and sky would evoke, then we have illusion. To a child, a rainbow is a real thing, and he may believe that he can touch it and find gold at its end. His disappointment in finding it to be cold, dreary drops is great.

However, to the mature person the rainbow is a beautiful illusion. He does not take it for what it is not. He feels its beauty as much as the child does, although he knows it is transient; but it has a loveliness for him which a child cannot appreciate. It is illusion but it has fulfilled its promise.

Life is illusive. It is an education, a training in strength of purpose and self-discipline. The reward we get is not the one for which we worked but a reward more permanent and deeper.

And so I say to a disillusioned young man that none of us can achieve a complete fulfillment or understanding of this strange, contradictory thing called life. It is good to have illusions, for without them there would be no ambition, no progress, no striving for what is better. That we must shed our illusions in the same way as we lose our baby teeth, is not and should not be a cause for lament. Disillusionment is not synonymous with disappointment. To all young people I say, "Delusion—no; Illusion—yes."

The wind is blowing briskly and the cards flap with the breeze. From trees and poles they wave, loosened from the strings which held them. The form of all the cards is the same; only the names are different. "Vote for X," they say, and in some instances they carry laudatory sentiments concerning the candidate.

An exploded firecracker and an election poster the day after Election Day are both inglorious reminders of something which has passed. The pictures of the candidates seem to breathe an air of confidence, a certainty of election. In many cases, high hopes have been dashed to the ground.

It may be asked whether the unsuccessful candidates should not have their posters removed a day or two after their defeat at the polls. Why have before your eyes a reminder of something you aspired to be and did not succeed in attaining? Is it not painful to recognize that one failed, and to see in the posters the leering face of one who taunts us? Psychiatrists today talk in terms of frustrations. They point out that many people are leading unhappy lives because they were thwarted in many of their greatest desires. To avoid frustrations seems to be the goal of a well-balanced life.

To me it seems that while frustrations may make us unhappy, yet a proper attitude toward life will prevent us from becoming warped as a result of defeat. How can this be achieved? The answer is that we must learn that disappointment is part of life's scheme. There is always a disparity between what we are and what we want to be. Our hopes and ambitions are always far ahead of life's realities. Should we succeed in attaining our goals, they would no longer be goals; and we should then be compelled to set our sights on a new objective. All of us, in some way, are like Moses who stood on the mountain and beheld the Promised Land from the distance but could not enter it. To accept disappointment is an essential discipline of life. We must keep on trying even when we know that we may not succeed. The struggle itself has its value. It is well to remember Arthur Hugh Clough's poem beginning with the line, "Say not, the struggle naught availeth."

Let the posters flap in the wind and let the defeated candidates see them. They may stir up renewed ambitions and may recall the memory of a valiant struggle.

Man's achievements in the control of the forces of nature have been tremendous in the last few centuries. In every domain of the physical world we have made almost incredible progress. Now, as never before, we look upon a world over which we exercise control.

In speaking of this matter with a group of people recently, I heard a man speak with pride of our mastery of the universe. Surely this is something of which to be proud. The speaker, however, like many others, failed to understand that this alone is not the whole of life. Holding the forces of nature in our hands is not an automatic assurance that thereby we will attain happiness. It should be understood that often we are better off not by mastering forces but rather through being mastered by them. Some of the greatest contributions to human welfare have been made by those who were not masters of but slaves to a great ideal.

You need but look at a great musician, an artist, or a scientist. Of such people it can be said, not that they mastered their branch of learning, but rather that it mastered them. Upon the altar of their great interest, they are willing to sacrifice comforts, tranquility, often even life itself.

A person like Toscanini can be more truly said to have been mastered by music than to have mastered it. He was its slave. The same thing applies to an artist like Van Gogh, and it is also the test of a truly religious person. To be a servant of a great ideal is no disgrace. Standing before the Ark on the Sabbath, the Jew says, "I am the servant of the Holy One, blessed be He." To be so carried away by a great emotion as to completely lose oneself in it, is to attain happiness. One may like to swim and master the waves, yet it is a delight sometimes to yield oneself to the water and to allow it to carry you.

There are, of course, people who believe in being rational and circumspect in everything they do. They believe that everything in life should be taken casually and that one must be in complete control of a situation at all times. At Shevuos time, our ancestors stood at Mt. Sinai. If they had been completely rational, it is questionable if they would have so avidly accepted the Torah, with all its responsibilities. But they were filled with religious fervor and cried out, "We will do and hear." Observe that first they pledged themselves to act and then to reason about it.

Life without enthusiasm is pale and dull. But what do we mean by enthusiasm? The word in its original Greek meaning denotes, "being possessed by God," i.e., being mastered by godliness.

We often hear people say to one who is eager about a project, "Don't go overboard." But if you're in a boat you will not be able to swim if you don't go overboard. A rational understanding of the forces of life may give us mastery, but a sensitive appreciation of them will impress us with life's mystery.

It is not always good to be a master. It often helps to be a servant.

A series of articles in *The New York Times*, during the past week, describes the use of drugs, by adolescents and adults, by men and women, by misfits in the social order and by highly successful individuals, by white people as well as by others.

This carefully documented study should serve to negate some widely held misconceptions. It is not true, for instance, that people resort to drugs in order to forget their troubles or ease their pains. It is not true that poverty and slums are the sole causes of drug addiction.

The fundamental idea is that people find life boring and existence seems purposeless. Consciousness of death troubles people now more than it did in the past. For, in days gone by, there were those for whom death meant the beginning of a new kind of life, more glorious than any earthly existence. For others, death meant a blessed release from affliction. For a great many people who cherished no hope of a future existence, the brevity of life constituted a challenge to get things done. This spirit is expressed in the words of the *Ethics of the Fathers*, "The day is short, the work is great, and the Master is pressing the workers."

In former generations, one who died did not have as much to leave behind as one who dies now. With all the comforts, the gadgets, and the pleasures of today's world, no wonder that men are loath to die. People seek to escape the awareness of death. By means of drugs, they transport themselves to the outer realms of their emotions, trying to make a landing on some unknown planet of themselves.

With so much that remains to be done, people evade responsibility by escaping from reality. Some vague absorption into a meditative state, some loosely used words whose exact meaning the speaker himself doesn't understand, Indian yogis who say, "The secret of life is the basis of life," a pseudo-mystical justification of what would seem obnoxious if said in ordinary language—these are the elements in an effort to stop the world and let people get off.

For a perceptive and sensitive person, life need never be dull. The unknown ways of nature, the secrets of the sea, the probing of the pathways of the heavens, outside the ineffable mystery of love, the sigh of the desperate, the grinding poverty of the underprivileged, the yearning for peace—how challenging all of these should be to an intelligent human being.

If life is purposeless, if it lacks significance, surely the way to give it meaning is not by putting oneself, through drugs or liquor, into a state where it makes no difference whether life is or is not meaningful. To give purpose to life, one must stay here on earth.

The effects of our scientific age, and of the automation which is characteristic of our time, are to be seen not only in the material improvement of the world but also in the psychological impact upon all of us. We have become accustomed to searching for cause and effect. We explain the actions of human beings by hereditary strains or environmental factors. Anti-social conduct is explained by citing economic and social conditions under which people live. There seems to be an almost complete obliteration of the idea of personal responsibility.

In ancient times, it was believed that the star under which one was born determined his destiny. Astrology was a convenient device for evading responsibility. Shakespeare puts into the mouth of one of his characters, Cassius, in *Julius Caesar,* the statement: "The fault, dear Brutus, is not in our stars, But in ourselves, that we are underlings." This is a truth which Judaism has always emphasized. The rabbis say that there is no dependence on stars in Jewish belief.

This is an important lesson for the contemporary world, in which determinism seems to hold sway. There is a feeling that we are the helpless and hapless victims of outside forces which manipulate us. With such a concept, the sense of wrongdoing is weakened and a judgment of guilt becomes well-nigh impossible.

But this attitude influences not only our conduct but our inner feeling as well. More and more do we attach to external things almost complete sway over our happiness. We feel we can be happy only if we possess certain objects or enjoy certain luxuries. The truth of the matter is that we and we alone determine what effect external things will have upon us. It is good to remember that what turns "better" to "bitter" is merely the "I." A distinguished American once said that there is no such thing as bad weather. There are only good clothes. This statement might well be used as a slogan for disgruntled human beings.

Some paper is classed as a letterhead. It bears the name and, most often, the address of the individual who uses it. Other paper is just a blank sheet on which one may write anything he pleases, a convenient vehicle for anonymous missives. So in human life there are people who are able to speak with assurance, who bring their individuality into play while others are indistinguishable from the mass of their fellowmen and what they do is completely impersonal.

And there is one thing more which impresses me about the manner in which we write on paper. We may be careless with margins to the right, to the left or at the bottom but there is, or should be, a margin or room on top. Life may be dull or difficult, smooth or strenuous but we should never lose sight of the fact that there is always a margin on top, that we have a space above in which we can move and which sets off all the writing we put on paper.

Few people whom we meet in our daily contacts are so completely sure of themselves as to feel adequate for the strains and tensions of living in the modern world. On all sides we hear the complaint that the strains inherent in modern civilization are difficult to endure. Rather frequently do we encounter those who, at least temporarily, break down under the pressures and tensions of contemporary life.

Judging on the basis of history, we should find it easier to live than did past generations. Enemies, hidden and overt, which our ancestors feared, no longer threaten us. A paralyzing irrational dread of evil spirits and demons no longer exists. Nor do we have reason to fear the ravages of diseases which although uncontrollable in the past are now amenable to treatment.

During the past week, there was a conference in which religious leaders and prominent psychiatrists jointly participated. Dr. Karl Menninger, a renowned psychiatrist, asserted that in promoting mental health the forces of religion and psychiatry, can, and should, work together. This statement has important implications for those of us who call ourselves religious people.

Many people, faced by the tragic things which happen in life, the frustrations and misfortunes, "go to pieces." Feeling inadequate to stand up to circumstance, they find refuge in a sense of persecution, blaming their ills upon some imagined person or thing. There are others who find refuge in a dream world where the realities of life do not exist. For still others, their inadequacy is compensated for by a resort to boastfulness; and what seems like downright conceit is, in reality, a pathetic attempt to overcome the feeling of insufficiency.

For one who believes, there is assurance in the faith that we were divinely created with adequate resources for handling life. Truly religious people are convinced that they have been endowed with added strength which is granted to them in the

112

hour of crisis. For them, a greater problem is merely the challenge to greater faith. If one looks at the speedometers of most modern cars, one may be surprised to see that the dials are numbered up to a speed which neither city ordinances nor plain sanity would permit. Yet, I think, the average driver gets satisfaction from knowing that the power is there, if the emergency were to demand it. In Yiddish, there is a saying that the Lord sends the cure before the affliction. This means only that we are adequately armed to meet the situations of daily life.

If religion does anything for a human being, it must give him a sense of adequacy for life. It is our *faith* which must hold us together within ourselves. The work for "peace" *(shalom)* in Hebrew is closely related to the word for "wholeness" *(sholame)*.

The training of every child involves some problem or other. Sometimes the difficulty is a trifling one, and sometimes it is serious. From time to time parents will speak to me about problems with their children, and I have learned a great deal from these conversations.

When some vexing problem arises, when something goes wrong, it is not unusual for a parent to say, "It's all my fault. I've been a failure." This assumption of guilt for the misdeeds of another is perhaps an attempt on the part of the parent to shield the child. It is equivalent to a declaration that the child can do no wrong, and if he does, it is not his fault.

Let us make up our minds that despite our best efforts, things may go wrong. Why this should be so is still a mystery. All the literature on child guidance and on the principles of psychiatry cannot explain why one child in a family is well-behaved and studious while his brother or sister is constantly in hot water and indifferent to schoolwork. This does not mean that the second child is bad. We are born with certain hereditary traits; and while some people use their talents constructively, others utilize them for evil ends.

Modern parents attend lectures, participate in workshops, read books and go to classes in an earnest effort to understand their children. This is most praiseworthy, but one must not expect it to solve all the problems which arise in child training. Understanding why a child acts in a certain way is one thing, but this does not mean that we can completely fathom the mystery of a child's personality. We must not feel guilty if things go wrong. We owe our children love and the best guidance we can give them. Then we must sit down and pray that everything will turn out well.

In his epic poem *Hermann und Dorothea*, the great Goethe dealt indirectly with this theme. A stern father upbraids his son who is about to make a marriage of which the father disapproves.

114

The "good and intelligent mother" speaks to her husband:

> We have no power to fashion our children as suits our fancy;
> As they are given by God, we so must have them and love them;
> Teach them as best we can, and let each of them follow his nature.
> One will have talents of one sort, and different talents another.
> Everyone uses his own, in his own individual fashion

These words can be read with profit by many of our distressed parents. Statistics can easily convince us that most children turn out well despite their youthful problems.

Most of us are so much concerned with our daily pursuits that we have very little time to think of our real selves. How often do we pause to think of the complexities of human nature, of the motivation of our conduct, of what essentially we are?

In the kindergarten, I saw a little boy accidentally jostle one of his classmates. I am certain that it was more an injury to his pride than his person which caused the "injured" little fellow to cry. I tried to appease him by saying, "It was an accident. I'm sure he didn't mean to do it." But I was not persuasive because he kept repeating, "I know he did it on purpose."

I began to think about the implications of this insignificant incident. How did this little fellow know that he had been hurt intentionally? Was there any pre-existing ill will between the two children? There was none of which the teachers or I were aware. Yet here was a youngster, implicitly claiming to know what was going on in another's mind.

Adults follow this same pattern. In some way, all of us, with few exceptions, assume a knowledge of the mental and emotional elements which make others speak and act in a certain way. On the basis of our assumptions, we judge and condemn our fellowmen.

Yet, even a moment's reflection should make it clear that we cannot possibly know what goes on in the hearts and heads of others. How much do we really understand of the dreams, the ambitions, the struggles, and the heartaches of other human beings? What do we know of their frustrations, their inner defeats, their regrets and their sorrows? And when we pass judgment upon our fellowmen, may it not be that unknowingly we are actually projecting an image of ourselves onto others, attributing to them all the things which we feel within ourselves?

It seems strange that we should attempt to understand the

wellsprings of the deeds of others, when we do not even have knowledge of what moves us to act and react. Much of what we do springs from hidden subconscious depths within us, which we try to explain by various rationalizations, but whose true source is concealed from us. If we cannot understand ourselves, how can we read the inner selves of others? Are we not adopting the attitude of the little boy who "knew" that his comrade "did it on purpose?"

How much bitterness and cruelty in the world might be eliminated if we heeded the admonition of the Jewish sage who said, "Judge not your fellowman until you stand in his place." I have a suspicion that this meant that we must never condemn our fellowmen, because no one can fully stand in another's position. Only God knows what is in man's heart, and since we do not and cannot know it, it would be well if we were to assume that injuries done to us, were not done on purpose.

In a rather well-known passage of the Bible, man is compared to a tree, and the analogy is easy to understand. The trunk represents the parents of the family and the branches are the children. The falling leaves in autumn symbolize aging and death. A familiar Yiddish proverb declares that the apple which drops to the earth falls not far from the parent trunk whence it came; and, similarly, children will, with few exceptions, be close to the character and disposition of their parents.

The analogy of trees to men was forcibly impressed upon us by the devastating gale of the past week, during which many large, stately trees in our community were blown down and uprooted. Aside from the fact that the spot where each stood is now empty, the falling trees caused a great deal of damage to cars and homes. Once the trees were uprooted, the possibilities of damage were many.

A tree is a living thing, and so is man. One of the differences between them is that while man can move about in search of sustenance, the tree must remain rooted in one spot. If it cannot derive its nourishment where it stands, it is doomed to perish. However, even man, mobile as he is, must have his roots. He must be anchored to something. For all people this means having a faith in the worthwhileness of life and a feeling of certainty that eventually, despite temporary set-backs, the good will triumph. For the Jew there must be, in addition, a rooting in Jewish history, drawing nourishment from a hoary tradition, deriving inspiration from those historic ideals which alone have enabled us to survive. One who is uprooted has within himself the possibility of doing great damage to others. He falls across the highways of life, making it difficult, if not impossible, for others to pass. He interferes with the normal business of life and creates a problem for those who have to remove him. An uprooted person is a danger to himself and a menace to others. The essential business of life is to find roots in a suitable soil and thus to be a source of fruitful activity to oneself and to the community in which one lives.

What a remarkable world we live in! What great progress we have made in all departments of science! We're using up our natural resources at a rate which may threaten our very existence, we breathe polluted air, we bathe in water contaminated by industrial waste, our ears are assailed by airborne inanities, our eyes are affronted by televised nonsense, our schools are battlegrounds of teachers against parents and pupils, our young people are in revolt against established standards, our country fights an economically ruinous war far from home, our streets at night are a no-man's land for decent citizens, our uncollected garbage piles up in the city while human bodies pile up in Vietnam—we've made progress, we're civilized, we've perfected the art of killing, we've become steeped in hatred, and we live in fear of a universal holocaust.

Recently, as I thought of war it occurred to me that the letters in the root of the Hebrew word for "war" *(milchamah)* is *lochem*, which could be rearranged to spell three other words which can be used to define our responsibilities in today's world.

1) With different punctuations the word can read *lechem* (meaning "bread"). Instead of pouring millions, even billions into the grim pursuit of taking life, we should demand of our legislators and our President that more be done to relieve the abject poverty of so many who live just at the subsistence level, while around them is unlimited prosperity. Despite official pronouncements, we cannot have guns and butter. Let's have more butter.

2) The second word which can be formed is *cholem* (meaning "to dream"). We live in constant fear of the destruction of the world by diabolical contrivances fashioned by man's God-given intelligence. We do not allow ourselves to dream of a world in which violence will be supplanted by kindness and hatred by

love. To talk of a "new world" is to be classified as a utopian, an impractical visionary. To dread is to have nightmares, to dream is to have visions.

3) Lastly, the letters of the verb root meaning "to battle" can be rearranged to spell the Hebrew word "to forgive" (mochel). Many may claim that we cannot possibly overlook the misdeeds, the crimes, of those we hold to be our enemies. To ask that we completely obliterate the memory of wrongs perpetrated against us would be completely unrealistic; but we can exercise the virtue of forgiveness, we can train ourselves to pardon transgression.

To feed, not to fight; to dream, not to dread; to forgive, not to forget—these three things made up of the same letters as the word to do battle—define our highest responsibility at present. They constitute what an American philosopher, William James, called "a moral equivalent for war."

There are people who go through life with a feeling that they are being constantly persecuted. Around them they see nothing but the cruel faces of tormentors who are ready to pounce at any moment. Those who suffer from such feelings of being pursued at all times are considered psychotics, in need of treatment.

Jews have sometimes been accused of suffering from a communal persecution complex. We have overstated our martyrdom, we have exaggerated the number of slaughtered innocents, say some people. The Jew, it is alleged, has been so conditioned that he sees discrimination and persecution even where it does not exist.

That we have good reason to feel that we are hounded is evident from what has happened in the last half year. Even if we put out of our minds the memory of the Nazi holocaust and the long road of martyrdom trodden by our ancestors, there is enough in recent events to convince us that we are not seeing ghosts, that the path of the Jew is a rough one, that we are still the scapegoats of history.

When the anti-American, self-worshipping leader of France found it politically expedient, he went out of his way to denounce the Israelis for fighting for life. When the Russians desired to gain access to the Mediterranean and embarrass the West, they openly and brazenly equipped the Arabs with weapons and technicians and assailed Israel as an aggressor. What Russia did in the Baltic states, and more especially in Hungary, was passed over in silence. Israel became the international culprit. When Negroes, suffering from the exploitation and enslavement of unscrupulous bigots and racists, began to make a determined effort to acquire the rights which are guaranteed to them by our Constitution, the introduction to the struggle was a completely unfounded attack upon Jews. It was conveniently forgotten that Jews were not among the slave traders in the American colonies, and that plantation owners were not Jews, and that there was never a synagogue which excluded a black person from worship.

Now, when Negroes feel that their children are receiving inferior education and that black teachers are suffering from discrimination, there appears a wild, irresponsible substitute teacher, who accuses Jews of responsibility for the failures of our city's school system. We have been accused of dominating the banking system, the entertainment industry, and now it's the school system.

The monolithic structure of communism is crumbling, and the most articulate critics of the existing political systems are the young men and women on the campus. There have been demonstrations in our own country, in Berkeley and in other places. Abroad, students have rioted in Rome, and now revolt has spread to Poland. How does the puppet Polish government explain the uprising? The blame is placed upon "pro-Zionists" and Jews. And, while indirectly and unintentionally this is a tribute to the strength of Zionism to survive suppression, yet it is unmistakable evidence of the fact that whenever and wherever a scapegoat is needed, the Jew is found conveniently at hand. Economic reasons, political factors, international relations, cultural elements—none of these is blamed for a student revolt. The Jews are held responsible.

What should our attitude be? In the face of these unjustified attacks against us, we might shrug our shoulders and say, "This is the lot of the Jew." But, for myself, there is bitterness and anger. I cannot do much about Poland, but in this country I shall denounce as un-American bigots and rabble rousers, those, be they white or black, who would vent their frustrations and suffering upon an innocent people, who, let it be remembered, was the first in history to raise its voice against oppression and tyranny, against injustice and inhumanity, and in behalf of everything which served to enhance the dignity of man.

Superstitions are expressions of the fears and the uncertainties of the common people. Things for which we cannot find a rational explanation, which reveal no understandable cause, are attributed to luck. One of the common superstitions is that which says that one who breaks a mirror, will have years of bad luck.

As I witnessed an incident of mirror-breaking last week, I saw it in a new light. It seemed to me that the old superstition had some meaning for us.

A mirror is an instrument by means of which we can see ourselves as we are. A painting of ourselves may be flattering, a photograph may be touched up, but the mirror shows us to ourselves without any flattery or, on the other hand, insult. In this lies the great value of the looking-glass. It reveals to us all of our blemishes and also all of our good features. This is perhaps one of the most important elements in a happy life.

In ancient Greece, Socrates told young people to know themselves. This meant to be honest with oneself, and unpleasant as it might be to face the truth, it was the first step in living a sensible life. To the founder of Hasidism, the Besht, came a man who said that after all his many exertions, he realized that he was an ordinary, unlearned man. The saintly teacher consoled him by saying that this realization was in itself a very great accomplishment.

If we can see ourselves as we are and take steps for self-improvement, we can achieve success in life. For me, success means self-approval. If the whole world applauds me but I cannot applaud myself, then, despite all the encomiums, I am a failure. To be able to look at myself and to say, "I'm pleased," or "I know what needs to be done to improve myself," is to achieve success. When the mirror breaks and I don't have the means of looking at myself, then I think it is bad fortune for me.

The old superstition, therefore, has meaning for me. I am forced to conclude that when it comes to a mirror, good luck is bound up with a good look.

It has frequently been said that he who stands on the top of a mountain can see a great distance in all directions, whereas he who stands in the valley can see very little. This is true in a spiritual as well as a physical sense. Only those who are able to take a large view of life can truly see it with all its lights and shadows. The people whose vision is circumscribed get a warped and false impression of life.

One of the painful experiences of life is to discover how many small people there are. What does it mean to be small? It implies being concerned with trivialities, in magnifying petty things and making them appear monumental. The unmistakable signs of such an attitude can be discerned in the speech and conduct of people whom we meet in our daily lives.

Ask some individual why he dislikes another and you will be saddened by the answers. "He passed me by without greeting me," "His child quarreled with mine and he insisted that his child was right," "She acts as if she owns the world," "After all I've done he said very little to show me recognition," "He greeted me with very little enthusiasm," "She is more enthusiastic about Mrs. X than about me." For reasons like these and many others, we begin to dislike our fellowman; and, once having acquired the dislike (or even hatred), we seem to delight in nourishing our petty grievance. Every new contact with the object of our dislike seems to furnish us with additional fuel for the fires of hatred.

It is a sad thought that so much of animosity is engendered by such petty things. But one must realize that it is only small people who are motivated in this way. It would seem that having nothing more important with which to occupy themselves, people seize upon little things just as children can spend hours playing with bits of paper or string. This is particularly distressing at a time when the world demands big people of vision. The world needs people who can eschew pettiness. There is too much misery in the world to have it augmented by the hatreds of small people.

Driving through the Battery Tunnel and mindful of the regulations which govern its use, I was struck by the lesson one could derive from the situation.

The tunnel has two lanes and a driver may usually choose which one he will utilize. Sometimes, however, the policeman on duty directs in which lane one may travel. In life also, most of us have a choice of the lane in which we will travel. It does happen, sometimes, that the policeman, in the form of outward circumstance, compels us to stay in a certain lane. We may discover, after we've traveled a while, that we might have been better off in the other lane. But the regulations say that you may not cross from one into the other.

Why are you unhappy (and some people are truly unhappy) because you're in this lane? Probably because traffic in the other one is a bit faster. The difference will not be more than three or four minutes, but still you're displeased. Do these few minutes mean so very much to you? Both lanes will take you to your destination. Besides, you will notice that whereas the fellow in the other lane may outdistance you at the beginning, he will soon find himself behind a slow-moving vehicle and you will not only overtake him but even get ahead of him. What is even more important is the fact that at a certain point you will have the freedom to move from one side to the other without any restriction. So it is best to keep looking straight ahead, continuing to drive without being concerned about the other lane.

Is it not true that life would be less difficult and tension would be decreased if we could learn this lesson? We find ourselves in a certain lane, no matter what it was which put us into it, whether it was a free choice or some outward condition. We could be quite happy were it not for the fact that we are in a hurry, trying to save time which we put to no great use after we have saved it. What distresses us still more is the fact that someone in the other lane seems to be traveling faster than we are. It will help if one realizes that he may not get to his destination before we do and, in addition, he is not enjoying the ride any more than you are. If he had the tunnel to himself he could be driving even faster.

Mental health demands self-acceptance. This does not mean a surrender of ambition but rather a facing of reality. To take our limitations and defects, our disadvantages and difficulties, and to keep going despite them, is the essential business of life. Stay in the lane as long as you must and remember that there is a point at which you will have the freedom to move as you please.

One cannot always be in a happy frame of mind. There are problems and difficulties which every human being faces and they stir up the calm surface of our spirit. So I also was depressed and troubled as I walked on 42nd Street, thinking about matters which did not contribute to my happiness.

I heard the strains of a familiar melody, played on an accordion, and looked up to see a young man, accompanied by a dog, slowly walking along. He was blind and was soliciting alms in his tin cup. He could not see some of the ugly sights of life but, then again, he could not see the sunshine and the smiles on the faces of little children. In my heart I gave thanks for the gift of sight and I felt a little lighter in spirit.

As I continued my journey I saw a man whose legs had been completely amputated. He was seated on a very low little wagon and he moved along by propelling himself by cushions which were attached to his hands. In times of trouble we are advised to "Stand up and take it," but this man couldn't stand up. From the "sale" of the pencils in his lap, he was trying to support himself. Did he feel as low as he looked? I doubt it. He had accepted his misfortune and was living with it. Once more there was in my heart a prayer of thanks, this time for the limbs which enabled me to walk, and I felt a little happier than before.

Just as I reached my destination I saw the familiar face of a gentleman I knew. He seemed despondent and I inquired about the reason for his mood. He explained that a member of his family had been operated on that morning and the outcome was uncertain. I tried to assure him that everything would turn out right and we parted. For the third time I found reason to give thanks, for the health I enjoyed, and then the spirit of despondency vanished. I have problems but I also enjoy many blessings of which I am sometimes forgetful. There came to my mind an old Hasidic story.

There was a very poor rabbi in a small town who lived on the verge of starvation but who was always cheerful. He was asked, "Rabbi Mordecai, how do you manage to do this?" "It's very easy," he replied. "Every morning I go to the town hospital, I stop at the information desk, and ask, 'Do you have a patient named Rabbi Mordecai here?' When the clerk answers, 'No,' I leave the hospital with a smile on my face."

With the approach of the vacation period I have sought for a program which would embody the essential elements of a respite from the cares and tensions of daily living. It may seem strange that I found such a program where one would not expect to discover it, the Twenty-Third Psalm.

The author of this psalm speaks of lying down "in green pastures." This is the first requisite of a real vacation. It must offer us an opportunity of getting away from hard pavement, traffic signals, subway trains, and the shopping tour. It must take us where we see the handiwork of the Creator.

"He leadeth me beside the still waters." It is interesting to note that the psalmist does not see himself standing on the bank of a running brook, or a noisy stream. This is important, for, before man created the mirror to see his own image, he saw himself in the water into which he gazed. And, while one may also see himself mirrored in a moving body of water, the image is distorted. One sees himself best in still waters.

In the busy lives we lead there is no time for what we call "reflection" or "contemplation." The word "reflection" is used in two senses, viz., to express the idea of thinking or to convey the thought of an image. One cannot do any real thinking without looking at oneself. Then we see ourselves as others see us. It is the only way one can truly look at himself. But for this we need quiet and an absence of that turbulence which accompanies the frenzied activity of life in a large city. We have ample opportunity for looking at others but we get little chance to look at ourselves. A vacation should provide us with the means of assessing our own hopes and achievements, of evaluating our goals and trying to understand life's deeper purpose.

"He restoreth my soul," says the psalmist. As we contemplate the beauty and majesty of nature, we must realize man's unique place in the world. As a result of the cruelties to which human beings subject one another, we often doubt if we have a soul. Man seems to be another species of animal who possesses the diabolic ability to destroy his fellowman in many scientifically contrived ways. But the assertion of the Twenty-Third Psalm is that man has a soul. Sometimes it gets lost, and reflection helps to restore it to us.

May all of our readers be granted a restful vacation, with a chance for reflection and a restoration of soul.

No word in our vocabulary is more widely used and also abused than the word "science." Ours is a scientific age. From the laboratory have emerged those things that make our lives easier and add to our material comforts.

But these achievements of science have given birth to a certain attitude of mind which does not add to human happiness. We have acquired a respect for the things which we can touch, see and measure. We have become what is popularly called "realistic" and we scoff at those who still indulge in talk about such impractical things as poetry and emotions like pity. Most of our young people devote themselves to scientific studies during their college careers. Very few students devote themselves to the humanities because they have no "practical value." We are raising a generation of technicians, engineers, and experimenters, but we are not producing a commensurate group of poets and dreamers. This is a disturbing thought at a time when humanity is suffering from "heart" trouble.

We cannot deny the need for scientific investigation in promoting human happiness. But we must stop to ask ourselves what we're trying to achieve with our researches. Science is merely a tool, a means to an end. What is the goal? One may perfect techniques for healing the diseases of cattle; but one must realize that when he has done the job, all he has (important as that may be) is a healthy ox.

Are the things of which the poet sings, unreal? Can a psychological condition that produces acute pain be called unreal? Are sympathy and tenderness to disappear from the vocabulary of modern man because they cannot be accurately measured and tested? Can all of life be explained on the basis of certain biological or measurable psychological traits in man? What of the ecstatic vision of the mystic or the inspired dream of the prophet? Are all the troubles of the world attributable to glandular disturbances?

It seems to me that we are so much concerned about our creature comforts, that we have concentrated so much upon living, that we have lost sight of the purpose for which we live. While it is true that man needs food and shelter and clothing, yet he also needs faith and hope. Like Abraham of old, he still needs to go out and gaze up at the starry canopy of heaven in order to find an assurance for the future. It is well to remember the immortal words, "We are such stuff as dreams are made of."

There are many examples in history of the destruction of civilizations and states not by enemies from without but by forces from within. Gilbert Murray, the eminent classics scholar, said that the fall of the Roman Empire was the result of a "failure of nerve." Soul erosion is equally if not more destructive than soil erosion.

The increasing use of drugs of all kinds, particularly by young people, is cause for grave concern. The use of marijuana is accepted as normal and the experimentation with heavier narcotics is part of the adolescent experience.

Drugs which ease pain or create a dream world in which one finds escape from unpleasant realities, have been known for centuries. DeQuincey's *Confessions of an English Opium Eater* (1822) did much to stimulate an interest in the use of drugs but did not create the habit. I do not think that there is a single cause for the spread of the habit, yet surely, part of it is attributable to the manner in which children emerge from infancy to mature life.

Being an adolescent is not easy. The young person is trying to cope with the world as a grown-up and, on the other hand, feels his inadequacy and inability to do so. There is a tug of war between a drive for independence and a sense of dependence. But one thing is certain, that an adolescent needs to be made responsible for certain things. To infantilize children, to make them feel that they can have anything without paying for it, to train them in a sort of credit-card surrounding, is to deprive them of a much-needed stimulus to becoming mature. Children begin to feel that they perform no useful function, that they are superfluous members of the human species.

It is undeniable that there are individuals who resort to drugs (many of them teen-agers) to escape from a poverty-stricken, dirty, hopeless environment, seeing no future for themselves and feeling condemned to a never-ending life of despair. This is the reason for the plight of the hampered. But what reason shall we give for the condition of the pampered?

The recent report about a young teen-aged girl who is a drug addict is a very instructive example of what is wrong. When this child of a prosperous, educated family was asked why she chose to run away from a home which provided her with everything, she answered that she was tired of nice things, that she preferred to sleep in rooms infested with roaches. This was another way of saying that she rejects all of the things which make life so easy. Something within us rebels against getting things for which we do not pay.

For the "hampered" we must try to create decent conditions of living. For the "pampered" we must provide a challenge and present them with a bill for benefits conferred. How wise was the writer of the biblical book of Lamentations when he said, "It is good for a man to carry a yoke from his youth."

Some years ago a book was published with the title *Why We Behave Like Human Beings*. The implication is very clear. Man is an untamed animal, with the predatory and killing instincts of the beast. It is natural, then, for man to be bloodthirsty and murderous. If this creature, called "man," displays sympathy and love, sacrifice and unselfishness, we must explain his "strange" conduct, i.e., make clear why we act like human beings.

As we read the terrifying accounts of the explosions in public places, caused by bombs placed by dissidents and revolutionaries, we are challenged to ask ourselves whether man has become truly civilized.

Dissatisfaction with the social and political order has a long history. In every age, there have been individuals who were troubled by the injustice of the powerful, by the exploitation of the weak, by the curtailment of human freedom. History is replete with examples of self-sacrificing, devoted leaders who overthrew existing regimes and helped establish a new order. Messianic visions and utopian dreams are born from dissent.

But it is not alone the goal which needs to be considered. One must also pay heed to the methods which are used to attain the goal. These must, of necessity, differ; but of one thing we should all be convinced, viz., that violence, the destructive use of power, to level structures to the ground, to plant bombs in many places, with a reckless disregard of the threat to the life and limb of innocent people, must be rejected. And the rejection is based not merely on the peril involved but also on the fact that this reckless violence will engender a counterviolence. Liberals are becoming disillusioned and bitter, and the forces of reaction are having and will increasingly have a field day. The cries of "law and order" will become more insistent, and suppression of civil rights will become the accepted order. The refusal to allow bail for those accused of crime, or to set so high a bail that it cannot possibly be raised, thus keeping suspects in jail, will seem amply justified by the actions of a small, but vicious, misguided group. Fury is no substitute for reason, and bombs cannot take the place of dialogue.

It may well be that the move to lower the voting age to eighteen will receive a setback as a result of this murderous spree on the part of some undisciplined, disgruntled people, who are essentially exhibitionists, looking for a chance to make themselves conspicuous.

The bombings, the stone-throwings, yes, and the assassinations of recent years, are retail examples of the wholesale carnage in which our world is engaged. We are reverting to the law of the jungle, and to say this is perhaps an insult to the animals. We will either live like humans or perish like beasts.

Quite frequently I am drawn into a conversation about religion and I find myself answering questions of people who take the subject seriously and are trying to work out a rational faith for themselves. This is very encouraging to me. But I must, in all honesty, point out that there is something troubling in many of these discussions.

Too many individuals, in my opinion, are trying to be theologians, and their concern is with discovering philosophic foundations on which to build a personal religion. There are too many who regard religion as an investment, whose record of achievement and future prospects must be ascertained before one's money is put into it. As a prerequisite, such people want answers to all the basic questions of life, the existence of evil, the experience of suffering, the grim reality of death, and, of course, what is beyond death.

This attitude contrasts sharply with that of the Jew who practices the *mitzvos* and who has a deep faith in God and in a purposeful life. If things go well, he gives thanks for everything, and the ritual provides him with an appropriate *brocho* (blessing) for every possible occasion. If matters go badly, he prays that they may improve. For him, death is one of the incidents of life, and if he were conscious that his death was imminent, he would resign himself to God. He never loses hope, for to do so would mean to despair of God's ultimate goodness.

It may be said that this is a very naive, uncritical, unsophisticated conception of religion, and a learned person might agree with such a criticism. But the fact remains that it was such a direct, simple faith which was of real help to people in hours of adversity and tension and which gave them something for which to live. For existing conditions the Jew said *Boruch ha-Shem* ("Blessed be God") and for the future he said *Im Yirtzeh ha-Shem*

("If God wills it"). To act on the assumption that what religion teaches is true, is the only way to find tranquility in life.

Neither Judaism nor any other religion answers all our questions. There are many areas in which we grope in the darkness. We will not be helped by philosophizing before we act and live. Life comes before philosophy, or shall I say in technical terms that existence precedes essence.

What is a real, helping faith? It is the simple prayer of an unphilosophic Air Force officer, whirling alone through space more than one hundred miles above the earth at a rate of more than seventeen thousand miles an hour beholding the wonders of creation and giving thanks to Him who guides the destinies of men and nations and bestows upon man the ability to probe the mysteries of the world and find joy and exaltation in living.

A survey of the emotional state of Americans undertaken by a group of psychologists some time ago has been completed, and its findings made public. The results of the study are interesting in many ways, but there is one element in it which concerns us here.

It was found that one of every four people feels the need for outside help in straightening out his emotional problems. However, it was only one out of seven who actually received some guidance. Almost one half of these went to see a clergyman in preference to a psychiatrist. It is the people who come to religious leaders for help that interest me now.

In increasing measure, people are turning to their spiritual leaders for aid in solving their emotional problems. The person to whom they turn may or may not have had some training in counselling. But even a minister who has been relatively well trained is no substitute for the psychiatrist. As a matter of fact, the minister, priest, or rabbi must learn to recognize a problem which is greater than he can handle. He must be on his guard constantly, lest, with the best intentions, he do more harm than good. His ability in convincing an emotionally disturbed person to seek professional care, is in itself a contribution to that person's well-being.

People do come to us rabbis with all sorts of problems. What have they a right to expect from us, and what do we give them?

I think we give people some hope where nothing but despair seems to reign. To the individual who is emotionally disturbed over some blasted hope, one can indicate the co-existence of the seeds of a new fulfillment.

We can and should give to those who consult us, our genuine sympathy. We can make them feel that we understand what troubles them and that we appreciate the depth of their disappointment, disillusionment, and bereavement.

What is typical of people who have a difficult problem to solve or an adjustment to make, is a feeling that the individual's problems are unique. No one else has to pass through the same ordeal. From his experience, then, the religious leader can show that many others have faced and are facing a similar situation.

We can be of invaluable aid to men and women merely by supplying a listening ear. To listen without talking, to hear without looking at one's watch, to give a human being a chance "to get it off his chest"—this is an important service and fulfills a need of people who need someone to whom to talk.

Perhaps, above all, we can and do give to those who come to us, some kind of faith. Faith in what? Faith that there is a purpose in the universe, that life is worth living, that all mortals are bound to make mistakes, that life is not easy but is worth the price we pay for it.

To give, or at least to try to give, to people who find life's road rough, a measure of hope, of sympathy, of faith, is one of the noblest privileges afforded to any human being. Those who are in a position to do so, are charged with a challenging and rewarding task.

The world in which we live sets up standards by which all of us are judged. One need only think for a moment about the expressions used in daily speech to get an insight into the standards by which men are tested. In speaking of work one hears the question, "Where does it get you?" The great problem is to "get" somewhere, to succeed.

Yet, as we think of this matter, it should become clear that what we want to obtain or to reach, although we may not succeed, is a greater sign of worth and a better indication of character than what we get. By the things a human being wants, we get an insight into what he really is. I feel we would learn much about any person by asking him one question, "What is it that you desire most in life?"

Many years ago a book was written describing the conceptions of heaven and hell which are held by various religions. As one reads the description of the blissful life in the hereafter one gets a very clear picture of what the adherents of different religious groups want most. Tell me what heaven is like to you and I'll tell you what you are like.

Students will soon be preparing themselves for final examinations. They will be judged on the basis of the results of these tests. But, if there were only some way of determining it, we should also judge by what the student wanted to achieve. Was he content to pass or did he aspire to something much higher?

To me it is interesting that in the Hebrew language there is no exact equivalent of the verb "to have." In Hebrew one cannot "have" anything. When we desire to indicate ownership we say (literally), "There is" to me or you. One says, "There is to me a book," etc. Property, possessions of any kind, to a Jew are merely external accidents. To hope, to will, aspire—these are verbs which the Hebrew language knows, but "to have" is not in our vocabulary.

The failures in life are not those who were unable to reach their goals nor are the successes in life those who "arrived." There is a profound truth in the words of Robert Browning:

> For thence—a paradox
> Which comforts while it mocks—
> Shall life succeed in that it seems to fail:
> What I aspired to be
> And was not, comforts me.

The world may have its own standards, but a higher judgment will place the seal of approval upon humble people who are the glorious failures of life.

During a trip to New York last week, I saw a vivid illustration of a sentence in the Book of Isaiah.

The prophet says, "The people that walked in darkness have seen a great light," and this sentence came into my mind as I rode along Third Avenue where the elevated structure is being removed. Residents of apartments along that street have lived in darkness for over half a century. As they looked out their windows, they caught only a faint glimpse of sunshine; and when they slept, their ears were assailed by the clatter of passing trains. I can easily imagine the joy of these people when they awoke to find that the shadow had been removed from their homes. They could now see other people on the street below and were able to behold the rays of the sun.

The transformation on Third Avenue made me think of other and more extensive illustrations of light blotted out by darkness and of darkness dispelled by light. What had brought darkness to this street and what is it which brings darkness to the world? Is it not traceable to the fact that we have elevated the trains, and exalted other mechanical gadgets. These may add certain comforts to our lives but they result in darkening our horizons. We may well ask ourselves whether the loss of light is compensated for by the benefits derived from the gadgets.

This is a mechanical age. We are so mechanized that there remains very little for men to do. We have machines for feeding and healing people but we also have mechanisms for killing them. We have developed machines which are almost human, which can perform all sorts of mathematical operations. The day may not be far off when a sort of "Univac" will be developed which will be able to make decisions by pushing certain buttons. Will there still be any function left to human beings?

The machine has undoubtedly been a blessing to man in innumerable ways, and no sensible person will advocate a return to the spinning wheel. However, we must guard against the encroachment of gadgets on man's spirit. We dare not permit the elevation of trains to shut the light out of men's lives.

A popular, successful screen actor committed suicide this week and left a note in which he wrote, Dear World, I am leaving because I am bored. I feel I have lived long enough. I am leaving you with your worries in this sweet cesspool—Good luck."

The reasons which account for taking one's life are many and complex. There may be some who feel that they cannot endure the pain of a serious illness, while others are disappointed or oppressed with insoluble problems. Those who are tempted to kill the world may turn this homicidal tendency on themselves. What concerns me is not the reason for the aforementioned suicide but rather the note which explained it.

"I'm leaving because I am bored." To whom is life boring? Is it boring to men who, at great personal risk, explore the surface of the moon? Is it boring to the medical practitioner who is anxious to help his patient to health and to ascertain the cause and perhaps prevention of some strange malady? Is life boring to the poet who feels he has one more poem to write, to the painter who has another idea to put on canvas, in stone or metal, or to the musician in whose head a melody keeps dancing? Is life boring to one who extends love to others and receives it in return? Does life bore a parent who watches a child develop and who hopefully looks for the future to see what this child may grow up to be?

Life is boring only to those who feel that they have felt and experienced everything which the world has to offer, and that continued living is merely a monotonous repetition of what has already been. A more correct term for this state of mind is satiety rather than boredom. The author of *Ecclesiastes* said that there is nothing new under the sun, but he did not know that there may be novelties on the moon. No day is exactly like any other day, but one must have clear eyesight to perceive this.

Our daily morning service renders praise to the Creator "who, in His goodness, renews each day the work of creation." It was as

140

if the Jew saw in the daily rising of the sun the beginning of a new world just being created. The Jew's appetite for living was not jaded either by his afflictions or by the seeming monotony of his daily tasks.

It is extremely selfish, to say the least, for a person to bid farewell to a world which he deems a "sweet cesspool." A human being with a sense of responsibility might be engaged rather in helping to clean up the dirt of the world, the "cesspool," which all of us have helped to create. To spray the walls of our world with the graffiti of our discontents is easy; to clean them up is the challenge of life.

What shall one do to keep from feeling that life is boring? If it be true that one who has tasted and experienced everything has no interest in living, then, perhaps. we should leave some things untasted, unlived, in reserve, as it were. The pious Jew sought for every occasion when he could pronounce a blessing. Therefore, he selected one kind of fruit, which he did not taste all year round in order that at Rosh Hashanah he might eat and justifiably recite the blessing, *Sheh-hechiyonu*, "Blessed art Thou, O Lord, King of the Universe, who hast preserved us and kept us in life and enabled us to reach this season."

Life is not boring. It is people who make it so. At the beginning of an essay called "Is Life Worth Living?" William James quotes a wag, who answered, "It depends on the liver." To a Jew, to whom suicide is a grievous sin, life consists of an inventory of blessings enjoyed but also of a gambling on the untasted blessings of the future.

"There are three kinds of friends. Some are like food without which we cannot do, others like medicine which we need occasionally, and, finally, like illness with which we can easily dispense." This is a statement found in *The Choice of Pearls*, a collection of sayings by Solomon ibn Gabirol, a twelfth-century Jewish poet in Spain. He also said, "A wise man was asked how he became wiser than his fellowmen. To which he replied, 'I spent more on oil (i.e., the midnight oil) than they spent on wine.'"

How enjoyable it is to go back to the thoughts of those who preceded us and to discover their inspiring utterances, their sound advice, their incisive wisdom, and their deep consolation. Can there be any greater pleasure than to be able to roll back the years and to stand once more in the presence of poets and philosophers, of legalists and ethical teachers? This is made possible for us through the medium of reading.

It has been said that a book is a friend whose face never changes, and in all ages Jews have felt a sense of reverence in the presence of books. Therefore even the humblest Jewish home had a small library, and while the more erudite Jew studied the Talmud or some mystical work, the less learned read the Psalms or some form of devotional literature.

There is among us a code which teaches us how to treat books. One must not place a more important book like the Bible under less important ones. It is not permitted to answer the doorbell and leave a book lying open. One must first close the book. It is not permitted to sit on books or to use them for propping up any object. And when the usefulness of the book is over, it must be buried in the cemetery with the same respect which we accord to the bodies of the deceased.

It was Mohammed, the founder of Islam, who called us, "The People of the Book." This has been our heritage, and it is therefore no surprise that learning has held such a high place among us. In Israel, at present, there are more books sold per person than in any other country in the world. To read is to have one's eyes opened, to comprehend the vastness and the depth of those spiritual treasures which make us a unique people.

This is Jewish Book Month; and it is the solemn obligation of every Jew to buy and read a book. Let us prove in no uncertain terms that the "People of the Book" does not mean the people of the ledger.

A mother and her daughter were walking on Fifth Avenue in the upper fifties. It was Sunday afternoon. The daughter stopped and said, "Come here, Ma, let's buy ourselves a few things." The mother stopped with the young woman and both of them gazed into the window of a fashionable shop, whose prices, I am certain were beyond the reach of these two. Yet, obviously, they enjoyed looking at the clothes and jewelry which they knew they could not own. As I listened to their conversation and saw the joy on their faces I knew that they were deriving pleasure from this "shopping tour." It occurred to me that these two ladies had taught themselves a valuable lesson in life.

For many people, the love of beautiful things is inextricably bound up with the desire of possession. We insist very strongly upon owning the things we admire. Sometimes the urge for possession is applied to people as well as to inanimate objects. In the past, kings and wealthy merchants would buy for their own exclusive use the talents of great musicians or painters. Too often, marriages are unhappy or break up because there is a male sense of ownership. The wife is not regarded as the partner, the helpmate, or the co-worker with man, but rather as a human being whom the husband has acquired. It seems very hard for some people to learn that one can admire beautiful things without owning them.

We visit a great art gallery and admire the genius which was able to produce such breathtaking colors on the canvas or to delineate the moods of human beings. Is it a condition for the enjoyment of great paintings that they must hang in our living rooms? Don't some people realize that instead of bringing joy to one home, the works of art in a public gallery delight the eyes of thousands? Why are so many people unhappy because they can't take home the things they admire? Would we want to have a glorious sunset, a moonlit night, the singing of the birds, or the sound of a babbling brook wrapped up and delivered to us on our charge account?

This does not mean that we should not attempt to make ourselves or our surroundings as beautiful as they can possibly be. But we do want to suggest that instead of pining over the things which we cannot own, we should nevertheless admire them. Such admiration is food for the soul and it refines our feelings. A person's character can be judged by the things which he or she admires.

The lesson of the mother and daughter is a very simple one. You cannot always own the things you like but, unless you're blind, no one can prevent you from gazing with joy and appreciation on the objects you admire.

Unconsciously, we reveal much of what we are by acts that may seem insignificant. It seems to me that the manner in which we handle our morning newspaper may tell something about our attitude toward life. What is the first thing we look for as we take the paper?

Some people look first at the sports news. These are individuals to whom life is a game. They are usually the ones who speak of "playing the game," of "team work," of "being a good loser," of "striking out."

There are those whose eyes are directed first to the columns of stock-market quotations and business failures. For them, life is a business, a grim business at that. These are people who talk of "selling oneself" to get ahead, who speak in terms of "not selling yourself short," of "being in the red," and of "making a killing." I refer here, of course, not to the use of these expressions in one's business but to the application of them to situations in life outside of the office or factory.

Many people look first at the entertainment or amusement page. For them, life is an opportunity for diversion. They are the people who speak of life as "putting on a good show," "being a headliner," "playing second fiddle."

There is a group which looks first at the social columns and is interested in who was married to whom or who was divorced from whom. This group is made up of people who know the genealogy of society families, and who are interested in names. They can tell you into which families the sons and daughters of wealth were married.

We find many who read the editorial page first because they are concerned not so much with events, but rather with the meaning of events, the deeper implications of daily happenings. They also read the letters to the editor because they are concerned with what other people think.

145

Finally, there are the people who turn first to the obituary notices. These are generally not young people, but rather those who have come a considerable distance in life and see the shadow of death coming nearer. They are concerned not only with the identity of those whose names are on the death roll but also with their age. For these people, life is a serious matter whose inevitable end, to some extent, interferes with life's enjoyment.

So we have different types of people to whom life is a challenging game, a speculative business, a diverting pastime, a social whirl, an intellectual search, or a depressing spectacle. You have your choice; but if there is enough in it to keep up your hopes and to convince you that there is something worthwhile in the daily routine, then the periodical of life has earned its right to publication.

An expression that is used very often by modern young people is "to be with it." This means that one is not "square" or "up tight," that one is in line with the sartorial and ideological fashions of the day. These fashions are established by young people and are as demanding of obedience as any by Christian Dior or Women's Wear. That many (perhaps most) of the teen-aged set should be entranced by this life-style is understandable. After all, social habits as well as certain diseases are contagious. But it is somewhat surprising to find so many mature people jumping on the bandwagon and going along for the ride.

I must confess that I am weary of and even annoyed with grown-ups who desperately feel the need to be accepted by young people. They are afraid that they will be considered out-of-date, superannuated, bigoted. Subconsciously, it may be a desire to stay young that prompts the attitude. Whatever the cause may be, we now find older people affecting the dress and habits of the young. College instructors seek rapport with students by obliterating all differences between them. If a dais or platform indicates a difference between teacher and student, then, by all means, remove it. If the student believes in wearing an unpressed suit, his instructor must likewise appear in wrinkled clothes. For young people these things are signs of rebellion against the Establishment. What is it for older people? The answer is simple, "Man, you gotta be with it."

Of late, this playing to the youthful "galleries" (only the Establishment sits in the orchestra) has become part of discussions about religion, the synagogue, and the Jewish religion. There are even some rabbis who feel they must "be with it." We are told that synagogue buildings are too expensive and ornate, that those who build and maintain them do so because of their desire to display their generosity, that worshippers come not

147

to pray but to show off "their Cadillacs and their Puccis," as one insecure, pathetic rabbi put it.

It is time for some hitherto silent and timid people to speak out. There is a need for someone to say, "Man, I don't dig it." I still believe that there should be a line of demarcation between a teacher and the student. I recognize that the motives for synagogue attendance are not always the noblest, yet I prefer to see people at services on the Sabbath rather than on the golf course or in the beauty parlor. I think there is much that is wrong with the world and, what is nearer to us, with our country. I am convinced that young people should be given a larger, more responsible role in schools, in politics, and in the synagogue. But I assert with conviction that if I can win favor with young people only by agreeing with them in their negative attitude toward the Establishment and in attacking every established institution, then I will risk their disfavor. Speaking simply, I cannot bring myself to attempt to curry favor by eliminating differences. I insist on being my age, and I cannot promise that I'll always "be with it."

Part of the attack upon the Establishment by young people is an assault on the home and on family life. It is alleged that many of the evils that afflict society arise from the errors made by parents in raising their children and from the home as an institution. Left-wing students want to loosen the ties to the home and parents to such an extent that the home will virtually cease to exist. The baneful influence of that diabolic, pathologic, dietetic character, the Jewish mother, must be ousted from her role as an educator of children. Farewell, Mrs. Portnoy.

A recent study has revealed the dire results to the children of broken homes and homes with a single parent. In school, such children do not do as well as others academically, they are responsible for more juvenile delinquency, and they are generally less dependable than children from homes with two parents.

This was known to Jews from earliest times. History can prove that the two great institutions the Jewish people gave to the world were the synagogue and the home. Of these, it is perhaps no exaggeration to say that the home was the more influential.

It was the child's first school. It was the place where he saw the members of the family together, celebrating festivals and important occasions in joy. It was here that he beheld his mother who fed, bathed, and loved him. If there was one thing of which he was convinced, it was that everything his mother did was motivated by a desire to help him. The results of her culinary skill were consumed by a family sitting at the table together and joining in praise to God for His bounty. The child felt that he belonged here, that he was wanted here, that he was loved here.

Yes, it is true that his mother urged him to do well in his studies, prodded him to do his homework, and held before his eyes the ideal to which he should direct his footsteps. It is true that her great ambition was that her child become a member of a learned profession. Scoff as one may at "my son, the doctor," it represents the high regard in which Jews held learning. The

149

percentage of Jews attending college was always higher than that of others.

But now the home is regarded as an impediment to one's progress. The Jewish mother is anathematized as a creator of psychoses which cripple the development of the child. There is, it is alleged, too much restraint upon children who should be allowed to develop according to their own bent. Parental authority should be limited to making it possible for a child to do what he likes. What, then, is the home? It is the place where children hang their clothes and find the key to the car. "To be at home" anywhere, meant to be comfortable and at ease. Now it means to be unhappy. "Homesick" used to mean sick *for* home, now it means sick *of* home. Rootlessness and instability result from a dissolution of family ties and the break-up of the home.

The world may well learn from the Jewish people, which survived because father, mother, and children constituted a unit against which no outward force could prevail.

At the entrance to the Jewish home we place a *mezuzah*. This is not, as some suppose, an amulet against evil spirits, but rather a sign that within that home is a family, living according to a Divine Law which commands parents to love one another and their family and bids children show respect and love to their parents. Let me shake your hand, Mrs. Portnoy.

I was sitting at a table as a guest at a wedding dinner while around me people were dancing. As my eyes turned toward the door I espied him. He was standing very quietly near the door and he glanced over the happy throng. In his hand he carried a telegram for the bridal couple which he was waiting to deliver. He couldn't reach the person to whom the telegram was addressed because of the dancing couples. I don't know what he was thinking about as he stood there, but I'm sure he wasn't participating in the festivities even in spirit. He had come to deliver a message and he couldn't reach the person for whom it was intended.

Then it occurred to me that this humble Western Union employee was a symbol of something which had occurred innumerable times in history. Moses comes down from the mountain with a most important message, the Ten Commandments, but he can't get a message to the people because they are dancing around the Golden Calf. A prophet in Israel is consumed with a burning desire to communicate a message to his people. He wants to remind them of their lofty mission as a consecrated nation, of their duty to be an example of devotion to justice and truth. But the prophet stands alone in the marketplace unable to reach the people because they are too busy celebrating pagan festivals and too concerned with their petty pursuits. Examples of this sort could easily be multiplied. But it will be most useful to take an example from our own times.

In all honesty we must ask ourselves how much of a hearing is given to the person who has a message to deliver. Is not the preacher regarded as a necessary functionary and his sermons as intellectual exercises by which his ability is judged? Does the person who really has something vital to impart, who is eager to stir people to nobler living, get a chance to deliver his message? Is there not between the messenger and those who could receive the message a barrier of dancing, of lack of thinking, of the pursuit of vain things? The people take no notice of the messenger, and he stands at the door. Perhaps only one who delivers sermons is in a position to understand the difficulty of the messenger who has a message to deliver but cannot get to the people for whom the message is intended.

Children are sitting in a circle watching someone in their midst perform some feat. One little fellow who has arrived late tries to elbow his way to the front to obtain a better view of the proceedings, but he is stopped by one of the older children, a sort of monitor. Indignantly addressing the offender, he cries out, "Who do you think you are?" and then, "Where do you think you're going?" The late-comer meekly retreats and takes a place on the outer fringe of the circle.

To me it seems that the two questions that were asked are pertinent to the lives of all mature people. They are especially important to the young people who, at this time of the year, are being graduated from the schools of our country. We are so preoccupied with the small details of daily living that we often lose sight of the basic principles.

"Who do you think you are?" Do you regard yourself as one who is entitled to all the blessings of life without any of its hardships? Are you a person, who, in the hour of adversity, asks, "Why did it have to happen to me?" Do you look upon yourself as a creature who has a right to sit in judgment upon the shortcomings and perversities of others, in brief, to play God? Or, on the other hand, do you think of yourself as a powerless creature, an insignificant quantity in the universe? Do you see yourself as one created in a divine image, with the power to hope, to struggle, to sacrifice, and to live? One thing is certain, viz., that the kind of life we live will be determined by our answer to the question, "Who do you think you are?"

But having established our identity, we must then ask the second question, "Where do you think you're going?" It has been asserted that many of our young people have chosen the wrong road for themselves. It might be more correct to say that they have chosen no road at all. The difficulty, it seems to me, lies in the lack of purpose and direction, in the drifting without any attempt to steer a course.

The complete lack of planning for anything beyond the next day clearly reveals the absence of any ideas about one's destination. The hopelessness is expressed in expressions like, "What's the difference?" and "So what?" It is asserted that world conditions, the precarious lot of man in this atomic age, the economic insecurity of this age of automation, and the bitter, ruthless competition of our times, make of long-time planning and the setting of goals merely exercises in futility. But it is exactly this attitude which aggravates and even creates the chaos, for if we had a clearer idea of where we're going, we might set our faces in the direction of our goal. In the midst of our frenzied movement which we often mistakenly equate with progress, we must stop to ask ourselves, "Where do you think you're going?"

I was on my way to the city to attend a meeting and had ample time to get there at the hour set for it. A difference of a quarter of an hour would not have affected the situation in any way. Seeing a train approaching the station, I ran quickly, hastily paid my fare, and dashed breathlessly up the stairs, only to see the doors close and the train pull out of the station. As I stood there and waited for the next train (a matter of about five to seven minutes), I mopped my brow and learned a valuable lesson.

Why did I rush? I know that trains run at frequent intervals, that I was in no particular hurry, that if I hadn't run for that train I wouldn't have had to wait so long for the next one nor would I feel so upset at having missed this one. Then why did I rush? The answer is simply that I was a creature of habit and that I was following an instinctive urge to hurry.

The more I thought about this incident, the more I realized the folly of much of our attitudes and actions. Too often, all of us rush and strain to attain an objective, with harmful effects to our health, only to realize that we might have done just as well if we hadn't exerted ourselves so much.

Many of the inventions and gadgets which we use have as their chief virtue the fact that they save us time. But one might well ask what we do with all the time we save. You listen to the tale of a man who boasts that he made an automobile trip in record time, that he covered a distance usually requiring an hour in "forty minutes flat." The time saved is generally spent in telling other people about it.

What has been said thus far should not be construed as an argument in favor of laziness or sluggishness. We do not mean to infer that one should adopt an indifferent attitude toward the passing of time. When the ancient Latin writer said, "Carpe diem, tempus fugit," ("Seize the day, time is fleeting"), he did not mean that we should develop heart conditions in pursuit of goals equally attainable by an unhurried pace.

There is a Yiddish story of a man who heard that Rabinowitz's house was on fire. He began to run at break-neck speed. Suddenly he stopped and said to himself, "Why am I running? My name isn't Rabinowitz." When we rush thoughtlessly we may well ask not only the familiar, "Where's the fire?" but also whether the thing we're chasing is really ours or whether it is worth the pursuit.

To me it seems that one of the most important words in our language is "escape." It is used in the physical sense of fleeing from incarceration or freedom from danger. But is also refers to taking oneself out of some state of mind which is considered harmful or unbearable. A conversation I had recently with a lady into whose family death had come, emphasized for me the importance of the word and recalled to my mind similar conversations in the past.

Very often people who have fallen short of an objective, who have failed in a business venture, who face a difficult family problem, or who have lost some beloved one in death, feel that their problem will be solved if they go away. Sometimes they pull up their stakes and migrate to a new community in the expectation that this will remove the heavy burden from their shoulders. But too frequently this hope proves illusive. It cannot be otherwise because it is based on a false assumption.

The mistake lies in attributing to others or to our environment that which is attributable to ourselves. Actually we are trying to evade responsibility when we put the blame on people and things outside of ourselves. We lack the courage to face what life brings us, so we shift the burden. We do not realize that no matter where we may go we take our selves with us, and every person has to live with that which we call "I." The tendency to "get away from it all" is merely a futile attempt to take a vacation from oneself. The same moodiness or despair follows us wherever we go. We can be in the midst of a rejoicing throng and yet not be part of it. In an atmosphere of gaiety we can be alone with ourselves.

All of this does not mean that people who have been under a heavy strain should not take a vacation. Away from routine cares and petty annoyances, we may gain a saner view of people and the world. But this does not mean that we will in this manner eleminate the necessity of standing up to life and facing it, grim and difficult as that may sometimes be. The late Chief Rabbi of Great Britain, Dr. Hertz, once explained that when mourners' clothes are rent (kriah), they must stand to show that even death must be taken standing up.

We cannot escape from ourselves, yet people seem to run farthest and fastest when they are running away from themselves. To attempt to be master over outward circumstances and to admit to ourselves that we are cowardly in running away is an essential part of the discipline of life.

155

Wait a few minutes, Debbie. I can't read you a story now. You see I have a pencil in my hand and I'm listening to the radio. This is very important and I'll tell you about it soon. Listen! "Argentina, yes; Brazil, yes, etc." (After a few minutes). I count. One absent, ten not voting, thirteen against, thirty-three in favor. We've won. Thank God. This is a very great moment in the life of Jews wherever they may be.

Now that it's all over, I'll explain it to you. We Jews once had a home, a land. We were very happy there until we were driven out of it. For a long, long time we have been wandering all over the world, and have been chased from one place to the other. We suffered hunger and sickness. Many of our brothers and sisters died because of the cruel people who hurt them. But in all these long years we hoped and prayed and wept that we might live to see our home given back to us.

It has happened just a few minutes ago. In a place called Flushing Meadows men from all over the world have just decided that we should get our country back. From now on we believe that the housing shortage for the Jewish people is ended. Tonight there are going to be many celebrations, singing and dancing, here and in other countries. Tonight little girls like you, Debbie, and little boys will be very happy. Soon they will have food like you have and clothes to wear and toys to play with. Many of them have been living in broken-down shacks since they were born. Their daddies and mommies haven't smiled at them. No, it's not because they don't love their children but because they didn't know what was going to happen to them. Tonight in a place called Cyprus where children like you and their parents have lived behind wire fences, like the animals you saw in the zoo, there is singing. The fences will be removed and they will soon go to Palestine where Jews are free, where they dance the Hora and where they sing "Havah Nagilah" like you do.

156

You remember what I said tonight when I recited Havdalah. We thanked God who divides the darkness from the light. The news that has just come to us divides the darkness of over 1,800 years from the light which now shines for us.

Oh yes! I almost forgot about the story you wanted me to read. You want to hear about Cinderella. Well, we Jews were like her. We were hated and sneered at. For long years, especially since 1939, we sat near chimneys. But now it's different. We'll have the same right as others to appear in public and to mingle with people, the nations of the world. Our Cinderella people is now become a princess. What did you say? Why are my eyes wet? That's nothing. Probably some smoke got into my eyes. Let's sing Hatikvah and dance in honor of you and children like you for whom tomorrow's world will be brighter since we heard that news on the radio.

Sitting in the midst of a group of people last week, I listened to the talk of a lady who seemed to have an inexhaustible source of energy. She was the sort of person for whom a conversation between two people is a monologue. But it was not the unceasing torrent of words which annoyed me as much as the subject of the conversation. It dealt with the greatness of her husband and his achievements. From the talk, one would be compelled to draw the inference that this man was the most competent and gifted person in his work. This woman is not in a class by herself. I have seen other people inordinately impressed with their own importance who lose no chance to tell others what they have achieved and which famous people they have met. Apropos of nothing they are suddenly "reminded of the time" when they shook the hand of some dignitary.

It seems so difficult for some people to learn the lesson of humility. Yet this is one of the virtues which is extolled in Jewish literature. The rabbis say that Israel enjoys the divine love because even when greatness is showered upon the people it makes itself small. Whenever a pious Jew achieved anything in life, he attributed his success to divine favor, and not to any special powers which he possessed. The Bible describes as ungodly that individual who claims that his strength alone was responsible for his accomplishments.

The immortal teacher and law-giver of the Jewish people, Moses, is described as a humble man. It is this characteristic of his which is singled out for special mention. In humility did he accept the task for which he was designated and humbly did he cast in his lot with his brethren, asking for no privileges and refraining from talking of what he had done.

Rightly understood, humility is the essence of Judaism or of religion generally. People who constantly talk about themselves and their exploits are unconsciously setting up gods which they worship. This is a subtle form of idolatry. The worship of a human being is opposed to everything which our faith teaches, and when that human being is ourselves we are surely guilty of the worst kind of idolatry. Boasting about oneself may be a fascinating subject to the boaster; it is a source of boredom and annoyance to the listener. Would that all people would learn the lesson of humility!

158

Last week I relived a chapter of Jewish history. I walked amid the ruins of what had been the synagogue and classrooms of a *yeshivah*. The pungent odor of burned wood, the slivers of broken glass, the electric cables hanging from the ceiling like outstretched arms, the black muck from the combination of water, dust, and charred articles—all of these were part of the mournful spectacle created by the baseless bitterness and dastardly delinquency of young arsonists.

But more than the vestiges of a conflagration were seen. In a separate room I saw the charred remains of Torah scrolls, damaged beyond repair, the remnants of *t'philin* consumed by the flames. The most touching sight, however, were the faces of rabbis (teachers in the *yeshivah*), moistened with tears, as they gazed upon these sacred remnants. Mayor Lindsay stood near them, visibly touched. You don't have to be Jewish to feel the reverence we have for our sacred books. I could not restrain my tears as I saw the learned head of the *yeshivah* point to one scroll and say, "This Torah is my personal property. I, and members of my family, carried it with us through the trials of the Nazi era. We were able to keep it and bring it here, to this country, only to have it destroyed by vandals."

I was reminded in that moment of the third-century scholar, Rabbi Hananiah ben Teradyon, who was put to death at the stake for teaching the Torah. A scroll was wrapped around him and as the flames consumed it, he was asked by his students what he saw. His answer is the challenge and answer to all who have burned our books. "The parchment is consumed, but the letters fly in the air." I thought also of the dirge written in the thirteenth century by Rabbi Meir of Rothenburg, when scrolls of the Torah were burned.

Perhaps the chapter and verse to which one of the *yeshivah* scrolls was turned was Chapter 19 of Leviticus, admonishing us

159

to love our neighbors, or perhaps the portion which bids us aid even our enemies. Which religious group is it with which the young arsonists are affiliated? Has their religious leader taught them to respect the faith of others, or has he told them that only they are the possessors of the truth and that all others may be treated with contempt? Jews have risked their lives to rescue Torah scrolls from the flames, and here we have the deliberate destruction of that document which has taught and teaches men to live in such a way as to prove that they are made in God's image.

On the floor, in the debris of this fire, were pieces of paper on which one could scarcely read the words. But as we walked on this floor, the rabbi who was leading us implored us to be careful lest we step upon pages from the Talmud which were embedded in the mire.

We weep as we contemplate what hatred and irresponsibility can do, but I was convinced in the *yeshivah,* and I remain certain, that a people which weeps over a parchment scroll and avoids stepping on a printed book is a people that is endowed with immortality.

At some time or other we hear a complaint from a man or woman which contains the statement, "Life has been unkind to me," or "I've gotten a raw deal." While one readily understands that there are defeats and disappointments in life, yet there is in the aforementioned complaints an underlying assumption that needs correction.

Most people go through life with the feeling that the world is indebted to them. It owes them health, sustenance, freedom from pain and sorrow. and a guarantee of happiness. When anything goes wrong, they feel that somehow they have been cheated. It might help such people considerably if they asked themselves, "What do I owe the world?" This would make debtors of them instead of creditors. It could come about only if people realized that life has a right to expect something of us in return for the favors which it grants.

Recently, as I rode in a taxi, I realized that as we traveled along, the meter kept ticking away, adding to the amount I would have to pay when the trip was over. Even when we were standing still, waiting for the traffic light to change from red to green, the meter continued to work.

I became conscious of the fact that a similar situation exists in the life of every individual. For the further we travel in life, the more we owe. We cannot, in good conscience, accept the things that life brings us, without being prepared to pay for them. Every step further along life's path demands an increasing tariff. Knowledge is purchased at the price of sacrifice, and success is attained only if one exerts effort. For every joy there is a compensating responsibility and often a sorrow. One cannot lose a child unless one has had one, one cannot lose a fortune unless one has had the pleasure of first possessing it.

We must recognize the debt we owe the world for everything we enjoy and must realize that life expects something from us. If we accept the bounties, we must be prepared to pay the price for them.

The age in which we live has seen the invention and wide distribution of various devices calculated to make life easier and to conserve human effort. One would imagine that this would be an era in which people could live more leisurely without the tensions of past ages. Yet, it is alarming to discover the constantly growing number of those who suffer from emotional disturbances, for whom the stress involved in daily living seems unbearable. Almost every day I find myself talking to adults who have some sort of problem and who seek assistance.

No sensible person will underestimate the suffering of those who cannot find tranquility of spirit. They are deserving of our deepest sympathy and consideration. But there are certain things they can do to help themselves, and even an amateur like myself recognizes the steps necessary to achieve even a partial solution of their problems.

In the first place, I find that many people refuse to face reality. They create an unreal world in which they continue to reside. They may live as if the past were still here, and refuse to recognize that people and conditions around them in the past are no longer here. They may live in a world they wanted to create but could not achieve. Unless these people face life as it is, they will find no tranquility.

Secondly, I find that there is a tendency to exaggerate the seriousness of problems. Many to whom I have spoken feel as if they were carrying the weight of the world upon their shoulders, as if no other person's problems were as grave as theirs. If only we could display to their gaze the heavy afflictions of others, the complainers might learn to see their difficulties in proper proportions.

Finally, there seems to be a tendency on the part of many people to cast their burdens upon others. They seem to lack the ability to carry their share of life's burdens. They seem to live in that period of their existence in which all their problems were attended to by loving parents. As a result, they are constantly looking for someone who will relieve them of the difficulty of making decisions. To such people one must say very directly and honestly that living involves a measure of frustration and tragedy. Unless one is prepared to accept life on these terms, one cannot go on living. To live as a human being means to assume life's responsibilities.

162

A TRIBUTE TO CHILDREN

On many occasions, children who are appreciative of their parents' efforts in their behalf, pay tribute to them. I want to reverse the process and render my gratitude to you, a child, for what you have done for me, and through you to pay tribute to all children.

Your anticipated birth brought inexpressible joy to a household, and the hour of your birth is one that stands out unforgettably in my mind. Lying in your crib, a constantly moving, usually smiling and occasionally crying little creature, you kept counsel with yourself. As a smile spread over your lips in sleep, I was sure you were communing with the angels to whom you were closer than any of us adults.

Weak though you were, you had us completely in your power and we were happy to be your devoted slaves. It is good that you did not realize the extent of your power over us. We began to plan for you, and to think of your future. Much of what we did and planned to do was undoubtedly due to our endeavor to fulfill through you that which had remained unfulfilled in our own lives. You should have the things we did not have and become that which we unsuccessfully tried to be. Your every sound became for us a language that only we understood. To others it was incomprehensible, but to us it was very clear. Perhaps love is the best preparation for understanding the language of others.

With delight we watched your crawling and then your standing on your own feet followed by the first unsteady steps. You were striving to be a human being who walks erect. In your childish way you learned to address us, and your growing consciousness of our kinship with you brought us unbounded joy.

Having provided for your physical well-being, it now became necessary to begin training your mind. We smiled as we waved you off to school but in our hearts there was a conflicting emotion. What was it? Not fear, I am sure, but rather an unexplained feeling that this was the beginning of your growing away from us which is an inextricable part of growing up.

The assortment of colored crayon strokes or water-color splotches which you exhibited so proudly, were treated seriously by us. You were our Picasso, you were our private Renoir.

When we had company we sometimes, unjustly, tried to "show you off" and you paid us off, as we deserved, by saying the wrong thing. You saw no need for being tactful, for dissembling, for withholding anything you knew. The world had not yet rubbed off the youthful innocence with which heaven had clothed you.

You strove mightily to become a grown-up and you resented the fact that one must wait so long for maturity. Going to bed at night was for you a diabolical scheme contrived by parents to get some rest from the constant prattle of children. Impishly you thought of every device to put off the hour for slumber. May this not be, perhaps. the unconscious desire of man to resist death, of which sleep is a symbol? Over and over again you used the phrase, "I'm not a baby any more." This was an assertion of your independence and incidentally a reminder to us that we must be reconciled to the idea of your emancipation.

You must begin to realize that one does not get in life everything one wants, and that one does not always obtain that for which one strives. Part of life consists of defeat and pain and heartache. But this need not distress you if you see it as a natural part of the scheme of things.

So, I pay tribute to you, a child, for what you have done for me in creating a new kind of love in my heart and a deeper understanding of life in my mind, for the affection you have given me, and for the privilege of being a parent. In the words of a great poet, I say to you,

> The thought of our past years in me doth breed
> Perpetual benediction.

May you be kept in health and happiness and may you ever remain loyal to the traditions of righteous living cherished by our people down through the ages.

You are the best hope for the world's betterment, the compensation for all our labors, the balm for all our wounds, the fulfillment of our unrealized aims, the mender of our shattered hopes—you are the most eloquent assurance of our immortality.

This is the season of the year when families are reunited. From college campuses, young men and women return to their parents with interesting stories of college life and with new ideas which they have garnered in the course of their studies. I am certain that many parents will be surprised by the changes which have come over their children, by the realization that the child who left home a year or two years ago is now a mature man or woman.

But as parents listen to their children there may also be aroused some resentment that these youngsters think "they know it all." The strongly opinionated parent may deliver himself of a harangue about the change which has come over the children. Such a speech generally begins with the words, "You see, when I was your age, etc." It would seem that years ago (if we are to believe parents) all children were good and were respectful of parental authority.

Let us be honest about this, and remember the sentence in the biblical book of *Ecclesiastes*, "Say not that the olden days were better." In an interesting will of a distinguished rabbi who lived about 700 years ago, there is a complaint concerning the disrespect which the son showed toward his learned father. The rabbi speaks with disappointment of the fact that on a certain occasion his son told him that he knew better than his father what to do in a certain transaction. Let us recognize that youth is impetuous, revolutionary, often irresponsible, and rather ruthless. Mellowness comes only with age and experience in life.

Let me not be understood as saying that all is well with the youth of our day. The impact of the war with all its attendant evils has broken down many of the safeguards which civilization had laboriously erected. Respect for one's parents is a cardinal principle of our faith and an ideal which has been highly treasured by Jews in all ages. But, on the other hand, parents must recognize that the profound changes which we see in our young people are the results of external conditions over which we have no control.

Young people must be treated in such a way that they may know that their personality is respected. One cannot ride roughshod over the feelings and convictions of young people without engendering a deep resentment on their part. We dare not hold lightly their problems which, trifling as they may seem to us, are very real and intense to our younger generation. Respect for personality is needed not only in this sphere but wherever human beings are in contact with one another. People may not always agree with each other, but every human being is entitled to that kind of consideration from his fellowman which will prove that we accept man's creation in a divine image with all our heart.

Recently I had occasion to transfer the contents of an old, worn wallet to a new one. This afforded me the opportunity of examining each item and of wondering on the value of the things we deem important. What does the wallet of the average citizen contain?

It contains money, which may not be the only, or most important element in life, yet is essential if life is to be sustained.

In most wallets there is an ownership certificate, testifying to the fact that the bearer owns a car, and with this is another document authorizing the holder to drive his vehicle. Here then is a symbol of our prosperity, tangible evidence of one of our possessions, and often (depending upon the make of the car) a status symbol.

Many people carry membership cards of organizations with which they are affiliated. These are indications of our desire to communicate with other human beings, proof of our need for association with others.

In the last few years people have been carrying credit cards in their wallets. These enable us to get on credit almost anything we desire—food, clothing, gasoline, airplane trips, and services of various sorts. But all of these indicate our reliance upon what we hope will happen tomorrow. Buying and living on credit are merely forms of gambling that we will be alive on the morrow and able to meet our obligations.

But a wallet also contains items of a much more personal nature. Is there anyone who doesn't carry in a wallet a snapshot of someone he or she loves? It may be the grandchildren, a wife, a husband, a parent, a brother or sister, a special friend, the faces of the living or the dead, that look at us from the wallet which one carries with him or her.

And there are some people who include among the objects in their wallets some clipping from a newspaper or magazine, a bit of prose or poetry, a paragraph or a few lines which indicate what

167

our ideals are, a sentiment we cherish, a bit of literature which has been chosen and clipped because we feel it says more adequately or beautifully what we would like to say.

These, then, are the things we carry with us and they constitute a sort of summary of our interests in life. Sustenance represented by money, possessions by a car license, association by membership cards, confidence by credit cards, the need for love by snapshots, and our ideals and unuttered hopes by clippings.

Which of these are most important? This question can best be answered by remembering that when one's wallet is stolen or lost, the overwhelming majority of people would like to get back not the money but rather those things which another person cannot use. It is the symbols of association, the pictures of those we love which are most precious to us and with which we are most loath to part.

A calendar change makes us keenly aware of the flight of time. As we remove the old calendar and put a new one in its place we realize that we are a year older. We travel along life's highway, swiftly passing various places, pausing for a brief moment at others. As one comes to a railroad crossing, a place of potential danger, one sees the sign reading, "Stop, Look, Listen." At this season of the beginning of a New Year, these three words may serve us well as admonitions and as a program for living.

Americans are a people on the move. Before legal holidays, warnings are issued to the millions who travel on our highways exhorting them to drive with care. But even if there is no accident, the mere fact that we do not stop at any time, affects the character of our lives. We have no opportunity to meditate, no time to think through the implications of our era of automation, of political revolutions, of awakening nationalism, of racial tensions. Hasidim who came to the synagogue for prayer always took time to meditate before praying. One can do very little creative thinking on the run. As a New Year is ushered in, we must learn how to "Stop."

Having done this, we are now in a position to look. We have a chance to gaze on the wonders of nature. We discover things which have always been there, in places where we had never noticed them. We begin to discern shapes and figures in the clouds, we notice the peculiar shape of a particular leaf, we are awed at the variegated colors of the autumn trees, we are conscious of the stars above us. During the year, we have little opportunity to take in the beauty and wonder of our world. So we are called upon, particularly at this time, to "Look."

There is one thing more that needs to be done, and that is, to listen. Most people are so busy talking that they have no time to listen. The air is filled with noise, auto horns, electric drills, airplane motors and radios. We cannot hear the sound of a child's voice, the soothing word of prayer, the chirping of birds, the sound of Bach and Mozart, the singing of the spheres. Our ear is not attuned to sounds which bring peace and solace to the spirit but rather to the cacophony of long-haired singers, whose admirers shout so loudly that they drown out the singing they came to hear. We need to be trained to "Listen."

We enter a New Year with all the uncertainties which are part of living. Our days may have been filled with tumult, speed and spiritual myopia. With a new calendar, may we attend to the threefold admonition, "Stop, Look, Listen."

It is natural for human beings to desire happiness in life. We would like to assure ourselves of a life in which there are only joys and no sorrows. We accept the pleasures of life as if we were entitled to them and we resent the troubles and pains as if they had no place in the scheme of living. Yet every thoughtful person will readily understand that pain and joy are closely allied and that one is almost the prerequisite of the other.

All of us have seen people who laugh so heartily that tears come into their eyes, and we ourselves have at some time experienced the feeling of crying for joy. The transition from laughter to tears and vice versa brings to mind the statement of Oliver Wendell Holmes that both laughter and tears turn the same machinery of the heart, with this difference, that while laughter is wind power, weeping is water power.

There are a number of electrical devices (of which the pressing iron is an example), on which one sees the settings for intensity of heat. One turns the lever to "low," then "medium," and finally "high." What happens if one turns to the next setting? Need I tell you that it reads "off?" From the highest degree of heat or power, one turn shuts off the appliance completely. One can put it in another way by calling attention to the fact that it is possible to change a funeral march into a waltz merely by varying the tempo.

Is it not true that the greatest joys in life come from the things over which we have been worried, about which we have wept? Can there be greater rejoicing than that which comes when someone dear to us recovers from a serious illness? When the psalmist said, "They who sow in tears, will reap in joy," perhaps he meant that only those can experience real joy who have sown in tears.

But the opposite is also true. We cannot and do not shed our bitterest tears except for those who have brought us our greatest joy. One does not deeply grieve for what is of trivial value. Only that which has brought us deep joy can move us to profound sorrow.

Laughter and tears are mingled in the life of every human being, and it should be a source of consolation in sorrow to remember the joy which was the precursor of the sadness.

Most people who have occasion to handle a legal contract read the provisions that are printed in heavy type but they neglect the small print. Yet, it has happened that some of the important details of the contract are printed in small letters. Therefore people are advised always to read the "fine print." I had reason to go over a legal document during the past week and was impressed with the importance of a thorough reading. But I also thought of the fact that very often in life, some of the most significant things are those in "small print."

The majority of the people whom we meet in our daily contacts are not guilty of any great offenses. We are not thrown in with felons or with depraved human beings. The wrongs which we commit or which are committed against us are generally small ones, but it is those very things that constitute the difference between crude, unfeeling people and others of fine sensibilities.

It is small things like a simple acknowledgment of gratitude for favors rendered, the ability to crave one's pardon for a slight offense, the restraint exercised while waiting in a line to be served, the thoughtfulness expressed in granting courtesy to other operators of automobiles—in these matters does one discern the character of human beings.

The tenets of Judaism are impressive and noble and yet, I think that the genius of our faith is expressed as much in small things as it is in the imposing time-honored principles. The rabbinic injunction that if there has been a hanging in one's family, one must not say to another member of the family, "Hang up my coat," or the command that the farmer must feed his cattle before he himself eats, express the Jewish consideration for the feelings of others, and even for those of animals. In small things is character revealed. Thus, as we go through the activities of daily life we should recognize that we must read not only the bold type but also the fine print in life's contract.

One of the greatest gifts bestowed upon man is memory. Through it, the individual is able to make past events live again. To remember is to brush the dust from an old volume and once more to read its yellowed pages. To remember is to hear the melody after the instruments have ceased playing. To remember is to restore the color to a faded painting. To remember is to replay an old record, with its ability to evoke tender feelings.

But the great boon of memory has another aspect. It can depress us by making us acutely aware of something in the past which it is painful to recall. It can make us yearn after that which is unattainable. Yet, even in the midst of dejection, there is an inexplicable joy, a melancholy happiness. To be mindful of the fact that once we enjoyed health and prosperity, that we had loved ones, should call forth a feeling of gratitude, even when all of these no longer exist. One should be thankful for the sunshine even after the shades of night have fallen. Perhaps it is better in certain instances to forget rather than to remember, but this is a bit of advice which cannot be given indiscriminately to all people.

There are three words in the English language that fundamentally express one idea. The words are, "remember," "recollect," and "recall."

To remember does not necessarily involve an act of the will. One remembers or does not remember without any conscious effort on his part. But to recollect and recall is the result of a deliberate exercise of one's will.

Life is disturbed and shattered by many grim experiences. To re-collect, to assemble the broken fragments of a sorrow into a whole vessel again and in this manner to re-call, to summon the past back into life again—this is the task of sensitive human beings.

We live in a continuum of time. The past, the present, and the future merge into one unending stream. What is past cannot actually be brought back; what lies ahead is shrouded in uncertainty; what we experience in the present is momentary because in the very process of living now, the present fades into the past. Rightly understood, memories are all we really own.

In the office of our school there is a large carton containing diverse articles—pens and pencils, notebooks, mittens, boots, sweaters, wrist-watches, glasses, balls, scarves, and even water pistols. Some of these things are of small value, but others are useful articles which are retrieved by parents who periodically come in to look through the "lost and found" department.

It seemed to me, as I saw mothers rummaging through the carton, that the synagogue is the place, particularly at this season of the year, where one may be able to find some things which he has lost. In the Middle Ages it was customary to pick up lost articles in the synagogue. What is it which has been lost and may be found with us here?

There are some who have lost heart. They have courageously endeavored to attain a goal and have had to give up the attempt, either because they found the effort too great or because their enthusiasm for the goal has weakened. To these people we quote the *Ethics of the Fathers,* "It is not incumbent upon you to finish the work, but neither are you free to quit the work." Success is often measured not by the achievement but by the character of the effort.

There are individuals who have lost face. They have fallen in the esteem of their fellowmen and this is a source of concern. To them we say, "Remember that every human being is created in the divine image." Losing face in the opinion of others is unimportant because the standards by which they judge may be unworthy ones. What is important is not to lose face in your own opinion, not to lose your self-respect. Hillel said, "If I am not for myself, who will be for me?" It is this one proffers to those who have lost face.

There are some persons who have lost their balance. Life, in large measure, means the ability to walk a tight rope, to preserve that balance which alone makes it possible for us to progress.

Numerous are the biblical and rabbinic admonitions to avoid extremes. *Ecclesiastes* advises, "Do not be pious overmuch." The rabbis say, "Do not weep excessively," and "If you grasp too much you will hold nothing." If we can only learn to see that good and evil, the beautiful and the ugly in life are elements in a composite picture, we shall know better how to use our opportunities and blessings to achieve balance.

But in finding in the synagogue things that we have lost, there is also something which we must lose there—ourselves. No life is significant unless and until we are able to find something which is greater than even life itself. In other words, we must lose ourselves in something very worthwhile such as our faith, our tradition, our devotion to the welfare of our fellowmen.

At this sacred season of the year, as we take stock of ourselves, we must find the "heart" we have lost, the "face" we have been deprived of, the balance which has disappeared, but we must lose ourselves in those things which, because they will outlast us, give meaning to our rather brief existence.

TIME

As I was being carried upward on an escalator in a department store, I happened to see below me an impatient customer who was taking two steps at a time as the contrivance moved. He could not wait until the escalator carried him to the floor he wanted. If the purpose of the machine is to spare people the strain of climbing stairs, then it was useless so far as this man was concerned. Why, then, did he use it? The answer is that he wanted to pay tribute to its value while setting his own pace. This man is a symbol of our civilization and is typical of many whom we meet daily.

Life, like the world itself, is constantly moving. The conditions under which we work determine the pace at which we can progress. But, there are people who are impatient and who want to reach their goals more quickly. For them it does not suffice to travel steadily toward an appointed goal. In their efforts to rectify the evils of society, they use radical methods, because in that way they will attain the desired results in shorter time. But the pace of social progress cannot be unduly accelerated. And, even·if this were possible, it would take its toll in the impaired health of those who rush.

We see the same attitude at work in the lives of growing children. They forget that nature has ordained that only the process of time can bring a human being to maturity. But our young people want desperately to hasten the process. They pull open a rosebud and want, at will, to extract a full-grown rose. They do not seem to realize that the processes of nature cannot be hurried. It is only unscrupulous charlatans who can produce "genuine" eighteenth century "antiques" in a few hours. Nature is not a charlatan.

Life's escalator moves at a certain speed and, while it is true that we can travel faster by climbing the moving steps, we do so at our peril. In matters which concern others, our attitude may do great harm to the social group of which we are members.

Istood in the station waiting for a train. One approached, but instead of stopping, it ran right by the local station. It was an express train running on the local tracks. It was an insignificant incident, but it aroused a strange thought in my mind.

Are not most people going through life, expecting the slower-moving local and seeing the express rush by them? We live and act largely as if we had unlimited time at our disposal. We expect that life will go on at a "local" pace and that we will have unlimited opportunities for doing what we desire. But, alas! life is running on an "express" schedule and hurries us on faster than we expected. This may not be a cheering thought, but it is part of the human predicament and we must face the situation realistically.

In the *Ethics of the Fathers,* an ancient teacher said, "The day is short and the work is great."

It is told of one of the saintly rabbis of the last century, that in the course of a walk one night he looked through the open windows of a shop where a cobbler was busily working by the light of a candle. The rabbi heard the cobbler's wife, urging her husband to stop working. His answer was, "I must keep working while the candle still burns. When the candle burns out, it will be dark and I'll not be able to work." The cobbler realized how fast the candle burns out.

This failure to realize the swift passing of time accounts for the disinclination and even fear of many people to make a will or to provide for their death. There are some who have a superstitious fear of buying a burial plot. Yet, among pious Jews, that was one of the first things for which a mature person made provision during his lifetime.

So far as our knowledge of the minds of animals goes at present, man is the only creature which is conscious of death. It is he alone who is able to anticipate it and, therefore, to set his house in order with his demise in view. We would like life to be long-enduring, but this is something we can't control. In waiting for the local, which gives us a chance to see the sights along the way, we must not be shocked if, instead, we get the express which rushes us on to our appointed destination in the twinkling of an eye.

178

Daylight Saving Time is over and we are now on Eastern Standard Time. The transition, which is achieved so smoothly every year, is an interesting study in the pattern of our thinking.

In the spring we advance the clock by one hour, thus giving ourselves an additional hour of sunshine (when it is not cloudy or raining). What we are actually doing is seizing time by the forelock and taking (or borrowing) sixty minutes out of life. Then in the fall we give the hour back to ourselves and as a result night falls an hour earlier than it did under Daylight Saving.

Is not this process true of life generally? Is it not true that when we try to snatch more sunshine than we're entitled to, we usually pay for it by having a longer night? The period of darkness and decline always comes sooner to those who are inordinately anxious to prolong the sunshine.

Among those who live in the East, in the lands where civilization goes back, not hundreds of years, as with us, but thousands of years, the addition or subtraction of hours is unknown. Time is continuous, and the yesterdays and tomorrows blend into a great harmony. The events of the distant past are for them as alive and real as the daily occurrences. While we in the West, in our desire to rush, talk of "making time," the citizens of the East smile because they realize that man cannot "make" time. It is as if they were saying that time does not change; it is rather we who change. Any visitor to eastern lands realizes before long that there is an aspect of timelessness that pervades everything people there do or say. In a running stream, one cannot separate the drops of water from each other and identify them, since they are part of the constantly flowing body of water. So is it with time, according to the easterners. It is an idea set forth in the psalmists' statement that in the eyes of the Lord a thousand years are as one day.

Perhaps we can learn something from the inhabitants of those lands which gave birth to the great religions of the world. Perhaps we should learn to judge time not so much by a western as by an eastern standard.

The pressure of modern life is so great that we do not, as a rule, have the chance to sit down and think. We are so occupied with activities of all kinds that we do not have the time to examine the purpose of these activities. However, like the weary traveler, there are occasions when we rest and meditate. Life is a journey across the calendar and we are made aware of the passing of time particularly when we realize that we are a year older. We understand that every moment brings us closer to our journey's end, and we desperately desire to endow every waking moment with significance; we want to lay hold of the precious segments of time, to hug them close to us to keep them from escaping even as we realize that we cannot do so. We cry out with the poetess, "World, I cannot hold thee close enough."

In Hebrew, the word for "years" and the word for "two" are spelled exactly the same, the difference being only in the punctuation. We can learn from this fact, perhaps, that the years of our life have two aspects, the outer one, viz., our reaction to what life may bring us. It is well to remember that all of life must be filtered through our personality and, it is alleged, that the noxious effect of cigarette smoke is mitigated by a filter.

As we grow older we become more realistic and we begin to understand what is important and what is insignificant. What originally seemed like a pair of tight, new shoes has now become well-worn shoes in which we feel comfortable. We come to realize the value of friendship, the joys of family living, the importance of patience and tolerance, the nobility of forgiveness, and the need for humility.

Growing older is dependent on heredity and environment, a matter of physiology and chemistry. Growing wiser is an accomplishment of the will, a result of a drive to learn and to think. The rabbis of old interpreted the Hebrew term *zoken* (an old man) to mean "he who has acquired wisdom." The great question to ask oneself on every birthday is whether an additional year has brought added wisdom, insight, love, and inner serenity. Wisely did the psalmist pray that God might so enable him to count his days (yes, days; not only years) that he could acquire a heart of wisdom.

There are occasions when isolated words bring to mind a train of thought which is completely separate from their original connotation. This happened to me as I read the obituary notice of Henry Luce, the successful and well-known publisher. He pioneered in the field of periodicals and produced a number of widely read magazines. His chief publications were "Life," "Time," "Fortune," and "Sports Illustrated." These words, arranged in the foregoing order, made me think of a connection between them.

"Life"—how is it measured? What are its ingredients? What are the standards by which we should judge it?

In the first place, of course, there is our consciousness of "Time," a recognition of the fact that every swiftly passing moment makes us older and gradually cuts down on the time left us to live. What we do with our time is an indication of what we think of life. Do we fritter away our days in uselessness or do we devote the hours to something which will improve us and contribute to the welfare of others around us? Do we find that there isn't enough time to achieve our goals or do we find time hanging heavily on our hands? These questions must be answered if we are to take a stand on the meaning of life.

The next thing we must know in order to define life is our conception of "Fortune." What do we consider to be real wealth? How much of material substance do we need in order to feel content? Do we say that health is our most precious asset, that children are our great fortune, that learning is life's most prized possession? When we say that someone "made a fortune," how much is that? When we talk of others who are "fortunate," exactly what do we mean?

Finally, I think that the complete life must have its share of "Sports." This word is generally associated with some kind of athletic activity, some competitive game, some form of legal wagering. But the original meaning of the word is, something which takes us away from our regular work, a diversion, a form of relaxation.

This, also, is one of the tests to be applied to life. At a moment's thought we can set down what people do for diversion. Some people prefer to be spectators while others want to be participants. The amount of money and the time spent in leisure activities in one city and in one day stagger the imagination. But in our individual lives we must examine what gives us diversion from our daily routine. Is it a debilitating expenditure of effort, an occasion for lavish spending, an opportunity to lose all sense of proportion, a period of tranquility like the Sabbath? What do we do with our time off?

So, Mr. Luce (or his obituary) made me think. "Life" is made up of our attitude toward Time, Fortune, and Sports. The happy life needs a sensible blend of these ingredients.

"L'chayim" ("Here's to life").

One of the subjects in the curriculum of our schools, to which students pay inadequate attention, is English. We seem to fail in preparing our young people to write correctly. Grammar has been neglected and proper punctuation seems to be relatively unknown. Yet, a paragraph often is unintelligible unless it is punctuated. It is the dots, commas, quotation marks, and parentheses which give meaning to an aggregation of words. And what is true in written prose is also applicable to life.

The hours and days of our lives are a procession of events, experiences, and emotions, most of which seem very often to repeat themselves in a familiar, monotonous pattern. What redeems them from triviality and insignificance are some shining events which punctuate the ordinary prose of life.

One recalls occasions like attending the first party as a teen-ager, seeing a sunset from some lofty mountain top, beholding the sun come up as one is borne aloft in a plane, standing in awe as one gazes at the Alps, or traversing a vast desert. But we are impressed even more by what happens to us through our human contacts. Who does not recall the day of one's Bar Mitzvah, commencement day, our first meeting with a human being who has a profound influence on our life and destiny?

Experiences like these give meaning to the unending procession of days. They are the punctuation which tells us where there is a complete stop (dot), or where one stops only to go on further (comma), where there are questions, and which parts of life, which, although included in it, are not really an integral part of it (parentheses). All of life would be but a string of words were it not for punctuation.

Usually, people go on living without a knowledge of punctuation and they complain of boredom. Often, people whose lives might be rich, merely pile up meaningless days. Yesterday, today, and tomorrow all seem alike. Shall we say that this is attributable solely to the fact that some lives are more interesting than others? This is partially true, to be sure, but does not explain matters entirely. It is, I think, closer to the truth to say that many people make no attempt to redeem their lives from boredom.

Over the life of every human being there hovers the spirit of high adventure. Life can be made significant if only human beings would avail themselves of the opportunities for fruitful living which are presented to us. For a sensitive person, even the seemingly dullest life may be made significant by the proper punctuation.

The tensions of contemporary life, which so often bring sudden death to many people, make us acutely aware of the brevity of life. Whatever the span of life's years may be, our pilgrimage is a relatively short one. We are constantly walking in a valley over which death casts its shadow. The grim reaper snatches children from the loving embrace of parents and robs helpless tots of an indispensable father or mother. He stretches forth his hand to sever the bonds consecrated through love and parts those whose lives have become intertwined with one another. To some, death comes with shocking suddenness, while to others it comes like the tranquility of sleep, after pain and suffering.

It is in the hour of bereavement that all of us become introspective. It is then that we seek for meaning and purpose in the welter of daily events. We recognize the inevitability of death and our helplessness to stay its coming. We know that out of the wreckage of blasted hopes and shattered dreams, we must salvage something. We pray that phoenix-like we may be able to rise again from the blow which crushes us to the ground. Wherein is this hope to be found?

We must understand that no complete answer can be found to the questions which scar our souls. All we can attain is a mitigation of the pain, for the scar always is left. And the assuaging of our suffering can come only through the birth of a deepened sympathy for the suffering of others, the attuning of our hearts to that which others are forced to endure. If death is to be thwarted of total victory, it can come only through an increased tenderness on our part toward our fellowmen.

Furthermore, we must seek to prolong the lives of those taken from us by death, through the magic of memory. To recall a work, a gesture, an act of one who is gone, to know that in making decisions we hearken to the advice of the departed, to feel that we have it in our power to continue the worthwhile efforts in which our beloved dead engaged—these are the only things we have to give us strength in the hour of adversity and to help us bear with fortitude the stinging blows of death. Life is brief, but it need not be futile.

What a remarkable thing is memory! It is the divinely endowed faculty of human beings to relive that which is over, the ability to find a present delight in a past joy.

Time passes relentlessly, and events rush by us in an endless stream. Nothing remains of the gladness of certain notable occasions except the memory of them. Once more we walk in paths we may never tread again; once more we hear the carefree, hearty laughter of children now grown to maturity; once again, in the midst of winter's chilling blasts, we see the shimmering rays of the moon reflected in a lake on some summer's evening. We dance once more at the Bar Mitzvah or wedding of a son or daughter. The song is heard in our minds although the instruments are mute and their players may no longer be here.

But memory is not an unalloyed blessing. It may also bring pain and regret. For our minds roll back the days and years, and with us, once more, are those whom we can no longer see and whose voices we no longer hear. We are forced to resign ourselves to the consciousness that the past is beyond our recall.

Under these circumstances we may well ask ourselves whether it would not be better if events disappeared in the sea of oblivion, leaving no trace behind. The speculation is an idle one, but it is interesting to inquire whether man's tranquility of spirit might not be better served if we had no memory.

To me it seems that it is best for everything we cherish in life to be able to recall the past. Unpleasant as the record of a bygone period may be, yet it is cheering to know that what is gone does not completely disappear, that through the use of memory we have it within our power to rescue from annihilation what would otherwise be irretrievably lost. To be forgotten is to die, to be remembered is to live. Looked at from this point of view, memory is the instrument which assures those who have preceded us and us, as well, of the blessedness of immortality.

The end of one year and the beginning of a new one is a period when most people take inventory. All of us look back over a year that has ended and gaze with uncertainty, and perhaps misgiving, into the year that lies ahead. It may be that the carousing on New Year's Eve which is part of American social life is subconsciously due to the uncertainty and even fear of the future. Thus, as we ring out the old, we drink in the new.

Much has been said about the resolutions that most people make as a new year begins. Cynics may scoff at this, pointing out how often and how soon the resolutions are broken. Nevertheless, making a resolution, a promise to oneself, is indicative of something noble in human nature, a realization that our achievements have fallen short of our aspirations, that there is a wide gap between what we expected and what we accepted. That a person, despite disappointment, can continue to plan and hope to improve his life is, for me, evidence of the power of God within us.

Regret is of two kinds, positive and negative. If one rues an action he has done or a word he has spoken, if one is sorry for having wounded the sensibilities of another by an inconsiderate act, word, or even a gesture, I would call this "positive regret," since it stems from something said or done.

But I feel that even deeper than this regret is that which arises from a failure to do, to say, or to experience, some joy, some achievement, some satisfaction which might have been. These are perhaps among the most depressing words in any language—"It might have been." Often this is due to circumstances beyond our control, but often it arises from our own failure to take advantage of opportunities which are offered us.

There were days in which the sun set in a burst of glory—did we notice it? There were opportunities to listen to inspired music—did we hear it? There were occasions when we might have lightened the burdens of some human being—did we

186

respond? There were times when we could have shown love to a fellowman—did we take advantage of the possibility? These are all instances of "negative regret," chances to add to our own happiness or to that of others which we failed to utilize.

During the course of the past year there were, no doubt, mistakes we made. Every one of us can look back upon some matter, large or small, which we regret. Remorse need not unduly depress us, however, if with it comes sincere resolution. Despite experiences of the past, we must still persist in measuring our deeds against our dreams. Life is never the total fulfillment of all our hopes. It has been said that it is far better to have something to regret than to have nothing to remember. May the new year see for all of us the lessening of hatred, the increase of love, the easing of tension and the attainment of world peace.

He blew out the candle stuck in a cupcake and said, proudly, "I am five." It was his birthday and he was understandably very happy. Then I asked myself a question. How long would he be happy on his birthday without experiencing a touch of regret?

As we grow older, birthdays become a subtle blending of happiness and sobriety. We enjoy the cards of well-wishers and the gifts of our dear ones, but we realize that we are a year older and hence closer to the end of life. We are acutely aware of the passing of time.

It is, of course, inevitable that we should look back upon the past, not only the last year but the whole of life. We recognize that we had hoped and planned and dreamed, and that while we achieved much, there is a great deal which was unfulfilled in our lives. The mistakes we made trouble us, the defeats and frustrations sadden us, and above all, we think of that which might have been.

There is no more imperious tyrant than a calendar. It is the outward reminder that we are creatures of time. The clock is the closest ally of the calendar. We realize that, unlike what is done in sports contests, we cannot stop the clock. This thought of our powerlessness might well paralyze us into inactivity. It would impel us (as it actually does to many) to open our morning newspaper to the obituary columns before we look at any other page.

Fortunately for sensible human beings, there is another way of celebrating a birthday. It is to be found in the realization that life is measured by only one thing, viz., growth. What is alive, grows; and what grows is alive. Time will take care of our getting older; we must look after getting wiser. We can see to it that each succeeding year makes us more understanding, more sympathetic, more appreciative of the beauty around us, more deeply touched by the afflictions of others.

Unless we are prepared to accept the changes that time brings, to be reminded of birthdays, we cannot live sensible lives. One of the things we do is to tear off a page of the calendar, after a month is over. Yesterday is gone, today is fleeting, but tomorrow is on the way. Every moment offers us an opportunity for learning, for expanding our knowledge of the world, for making the life of some individual happier. Very often there are brief periods of time which for us are suffused with the taste of eternity. Only those who can experience these hours, when one forgets time, can be said to be truly alive. Living, true living, is the ability to see and to seize the enduring in the swiftly vanishing moments. In the pursuit of this understanding lies the abiding significance of birthdays.

On the "Main Street" of our "village," there is a clock which is exposed to public gaze and is intended to tell the time for the passer-by. On several occasions I have passed that timepiece and have discovered, to my dismay, that the time is incorrect.

What of it? Is this such a serious matter that it deserves comment? Are your watch and mine always correct? Obviously the answer is in the negative. But one must distinguish between the watch which one carries in his pocket or on his wrist and the clock on a public highway. For the timepiece which I own is meant for my guidance alone. If it is incorrect, it is a matter which concerns me exclusively. But the public clock should be correct because it is meant to guide the public and, therefore, it dare not be wrong.

This is an eloquent lesson to human beings who endeavor to direct, advise or teach their fellowmen what they ought to do. While in our individual lives we may do as we see fit (and we are not always right), yet when it comes to the lives of others we must be certain that we are right.

This is especially true with that most valuable commodity of life which we call "time." If a clock is slow, it deceives us by making us feel that we have more time than we actually have. On the other hand, if the timepiece is fast, it is guilty of stealing minutes and shortening our existence.

A person's attitude toward time is an excellent indication of his general philosophy of life. There are many who act as if they had an eternity in which to achieve their life's work. They seem to have such a surplus of time that they find it necessary to "kill time." And some, who find it standing still, talk about "marking time." To me, "marking time" means to observe the all too-fast orbit of the hands of the clock around the dial.

It is a grave responsibility to tell people how late it is, because they are admonished in this way of the need to do things without delay. I have noticed that almost every bank has a clock in front of it. May this be intended to remind the passer-by that time is also money?

"Enjoy yourself; it's later than you think"—the music came blaring at me as I turned on the radio in my car. Perhaps the idea is one which deserves consideration, but I was not in the mood for it just then. I was driving alone, as part of a funeral procession. I quickly turned the knob and got another station, whose announcement is a familiar one—"The latest news, the best music." Now I heard the strains of Schumann or perhaps it was Bach, I don't remember. But it was inspiring music and I listened attentively. We're stopped by a red traffic light and after a brief interval we move on—destination, cemetery. Now come announcements, the "commercials"—a description of choice eating places, a bargain in a book on the opera, other announcements—then, more music. The procession slows down and now we're entering the place of interment. I turn off the radio. The service is concluded, the tearful mourners return to their cars, and I am now on the way home.

I begin to think of the deceased, of his hopes and dreams, of the fulfillment of some of them and of the others which remained unrealized, of the joys and the sorrows, the triumphs and the defeats which were his portion in life. Did he realize how late it was? Did he enjoy life because he saw where the hands of time were pointing on the clock of life?

It may be a melancholy thought, but sensible people must be conscious that every day of our life is a step forward toward the inevitable end, a portion of the journey toward the ultimate destination. On the way, we have our share of the "commercials." There are meals to be eaten and clothes to be worn about which we must concern ourselves, no matter how idealistic we may be. But, it seems to me that living a full life, a life above the animal level, requires that there should be some music, something intangible and non-material, interspersed between the "commercials." To recognize that Chopin and Schubert, Mendelssohn and Bach, have as important a place in life as the purveyors of food and clothing and gadgets, is to understand the meaning of a full life. To assert that Milton and Tennyson, Browning and Keats, are needed as much as Kettering, Ford, and du Pont, is to speak as a civilized human being.

The procession moves on—the "commercials" mingle with the music. The task of living is to mix the two in proper proportions. This job cannot be neglected—"It's later than you think."

Where does yesterday go? What happens to the days which have passed? Are they consumed as objects which are destroyed by fire, leaving only ashes behind? Is there perhaps some indestructible quality which can save the past from annihilation? The answer, I think, lies not in the days themselves but rather in us. It rests within our power to snatch the yesterdays from total extinction, and the means for achieving this is memory.

What is memory? It is the divinely bestowed faculty of beholding the golden rays of the sunset which went before while standing in the ensuing gloom. It is the ability to bear in mind the sweet melody after the instruments have ceased playing.

What is memory? It is the capacity to feel the zeal and enthusiasm of youth in the midst of the disillusionment and disappointments of life. It is the possibility of dancing in the heart when the legs can no longer move in time with the music.

What is memory? It is gazing upon the bride beneath the canopy and seeing the infant in the crib. It is playing with the grandchildren and seeing their parents. It means celebrating a boy's Bar Mitzvah and simultaneously attending his Bris.

What is memory? It is experiencing today the toothache and the heartache of yesterday. It signifies the sorrow in the present for an agony in the past. It is a conversation with someone who can no longer speak and the sight of a smile on a face no longer here.

What is memory? It is all that is left to us from the burned-out hopes and strivings, as well as the pain and sorrow of the past. It is that in which, above all else, is to be found the source of our immortality.

Mingled emotions are stirred within us as we return from a vacation. In thinking back over the pleasure we have had, in reliving many experiences, we feel a glow of satisfaction. Nevertheless, there is the sobering thought that part of our life has passed and that we must get down to work again.

I spent part of the summer in traveling over a large part of our country to the Canadian Rockies. As I look back over the weeks I spent on the trip, I am conscious of the fact that my sensitivity to the beauties of nature was heightened. Many things which, under ordinary circumstances, are commonplace, appear in a new light as we see them in a relaxed mood.

The overwhelming feeling which the vastness of forests and the tower-height of mountains awakens in a person is that of humility. Human beings, impressed with their own importance, lose much of their conceit in the presence of nature's handiwork. I gaze upon a towering crag and I realize that it looked down upon countless generations before me and that it will majestically look down upon others long after I am no longer here. No one can fail to be impressed with the feeling of timelessness that is born out of surveying the lofty peaks of snow-covered mountains. Keeping in mind the turmoil of daily life, we are soothed by the unhurried processes of nature. In everything around me I perceived what had been laboriously produced over many centuries. Nothing suggests haste or lack of planning. Glaciers on which I walked re-created for me the story of the world's birth.

But I do not desire to leave the impression that I felt helpless in the presence of nature's magnitude. I realized that behind it was the planning of the Great Architect, who has endowed me with wisdom to understand the secrets of creation and has implanted within me a sense of appreciation for all the things which could not be called beautiful, if the eye of people like me did not behold them.

As I looked upon the very high mountain peaks covered with snow and ice, I realized that if one reaches up very high and is far removed from the plain where people live, he usually loses in warmth what he may attain in height. It is well to aspire, but too high an altitude brings with it a rarefied atmosphere and a hard layer of ice.

The vacation is over, but I return a more devoutly religious person. I have learned the true meaning of sentences in Psalms which I had been accustomed to recite. "I will lift my eyes unto the mountains whence my help comes," and "How wondrous are Thy works, O Lord!" Truly, "The heavens proclaim the glory of the Lord."

At the request of a member of her family, I went to the hospital to visit an old lady whose days were numbered. Her children know that there is no hope for her recovery, but are doing everything which can be done to make her comfortable.

I found the lady to be mentally alert, to the extent of remembering the titles of books she had read in the past few years. For a while, she recalled events in her past life. Then I discovered that she had asked for me to come. The purpose of the visit was soon revealed to me.

"I want you to pray for me," said the lady. "Pray that I should die." As the words fell from her lips, I was unnerved. To request prayers for health and recovery is natural, but a prayer for death is unusual.

It became necessary for me to explain that suicide is against Jewish law and that a Jew is prohibited from doing anything which can hasten the death of any human being. This attitude is based upon Judaism's respect for human life. In certain specific instances it may be difficult to reconcile the Jewish attitude with the suffering endured by some unfortunate individual, but the sanctity of human life is strong enough to outweigh other considerations.

It is strange that the will to live which is so strong in human beings can be overcome by those who are suffering. And this must make us aware of the fact that the fear of death can be overcome. This is hard for most people who from early youth have been taught to be afraid of death. The black clothes, the drawn shades, the frequent hysterical outbursts—all of these have combined to make death seem horrible.

It would be conducive to greater mental health and emotional stability if we taught our children and ourselves that death is as natural as birth, that our appearance on the stage of life involves an entrance and an exit, that every play has a final curtain.

The pious Jew was trained to accept death serenely. Every night in his prayers he commended his soul to his Creator, and felt secure in the faith that whatever would betide him, would be in accordance with the Divine Plan. To be a Jew means to respect life but also to accept death.

Israel—This is my people. A people which has suffered and sacrificed, and fought and bled, and lived and died for the sake of an ideal.

This is my people, a peculiar, complex, mysterious people. It celebrates joyous festivals and ends them with memorial prayers for the dead. Its happy marriage rite is concluded by the reminder of an ancient tragedy, the destruction of its glorious sanctuary.

This is my people—individuals who have been accused of dishonest business dealings and who are commanded not to defraud another in the slightest way; a people whose constant greeting is "Peace" and yet has been accused of being bloodthirsty and militaristic.

This is my people—human beings who have healed the wounds and afflictions of their enemies but whose own members are persecuted and tortured by others.

This is my people—men and women, with the brand of tyranny upon their arms, hunted, persecuted, and exiled, yet finding few friends among the nations of the world—a people which more than all others is the symbol and victim of the struggles of great powers for world domination. This is a people which talks of milk and honey while all others talk of oil.

This is my people—a collection of diverse human beings, pitifully small numerically and yet able to withstand the onslaught of vastly superior numbers.

This is my people—storekeepers, tradesmen, and students who overnight become farmers and fighters, who transform arid deserts into flourishing cities, and wastelands into gardens.

This is my people—persons who constantly long for peace and are never permitted for a long time to enjoy it.

This is my people—which loses when it wins and wins when it loses, which must surrender hard-won gains against its will, but on the other hand is able to win the esteem and respect of those who appreciate determination and valor.

This is my people, a people which can look death in the eye, unafraid, and march to certain death, singing, "Ani Ma-amin" ("I believe"), expressing the unshakeable conviction that peace and brotherly love will eventually prevail in the world.

Yes, this is my people; and with all its suffering, I can affirm that I would rather be a humble citizen in Meah Shearim than a commissar in Leningrad.

One of the characteristics of the age in which we live is a desire for novelty. People want to read the latest book of fiction and to ride in the newest-model car. They furnish their homes in the most recent fashion, learn the latest convulsive dance, and have their hair "done" in the newest mode. It matters not that the literature may be of an inferior kind or that the styles and modes of personal adornment or decor of objects are esthetically repugnant, as long as one has the "latest."

This is not merely a passing fancy, but rather the expression of an attitude of our time which repudiates that which is old, on the assumption that we know better than did our forebears and that they have nothing to teach us. We scoff at their notions and feel that their set of values must be completely replaced by a new one. Respect for old people is an act of charity and not an appreciation of their value.

Yet, there is within us a longing for that which is old. Unconsciously we pay tribute to the past in a variety of ways. We scour innumerable shops in search of antiques and we exercise ingenuity in finding a use for them. We go back into the past for old songs and rehabilitate them, although we "doctor" them a bit. Then we take new furniture and hammer at it ("distress it" is the technical term), in order that it may appear old. Old farmhouses command high prices because so many people are looking for houses of a bygone age to remodel.

It is not my intention to plead for a return of what are called, "the good old days." The advances we have made in technological and social fields have helped immensely to make life easier and much less strenuous. One cannot possibly plead for a return to the horse-and-buggy era, nor for a substitution of the pony express for modern jet planes. But I feel that in our enthusiasm for the achievements of the modern age, we have lost a sense of appreciation for those things and ideas which have stood the test of time.

The advances in medicine are helping to prolong human life. The number of old people in our country is on the increase. Golden Age clubs and activities for older people now command the attention of social workers and political planners. What is being accomplished may yet bring back that respect for old people which our religious faith commands. We may still learn not to equate age with dotage, nor long life with uselessness.

Commonplace objects sometimes take on a new meaning if one is in a suitable frame of mind. For me, for instance, the ordinary parking meter aroused thoughts which far transcended the use of the meter as a traffic device.

The meter has been made to run only for a definite period of time. One places a coin in the slot on the machine and notices that on the face of the dial appear four words, viz., "expired time" and "unexpired time." Gradually the minutes tick away and the indicator shows how much time we still have left. When our allotted time is over, a red flag comes into view, bearing the word "violation." The law does not permit one to put in another coin and thus extend the parking period. It is expected that, when the period for which one has paid is over, the individual will move away and thus give someone else an equal opportunity to park.

I wonder how many people pause in the midst of their busy lives, to ask themselves how much unexpired time they still have ahead of them before the indicator reaches the end of its circuit. It may be argued that this is something which we cannot know. But it is certain that the minutes of our lives are becoming history even as we think of them. All of us are "parked" for a limited time only and we must manage to complete our business within the compass of that period.

An ancient Jewish sage said, "The day is short and the work is great." Disregarding this important admonition, people procrastinate and act as if they had unlimited time at their disposal for the performance of the important tasks of life. Over and over again I hear men and women say that they will study Hebrew, read a book, attend meetings, or come to services, "when I get the chance."

The meter keeps ticking away and, who knows when the red signal will go up. "Do not say," counseled an ancient rabbi, "when I have leisure I will study. Perhaps you will have no leisure." We cannot prolong the "parking" period. When it is over, we must move on to make room for someone else. If we complain about this arrangement, let us remember that parking meters are never placed on quiet, little-used streets but only on busy thoroughfares.

Last week, as I have done so often in the past, I parked my car at a parking meter and deposited the required dime. I knew that I had one hour in which to transact my business. But as I walked away from the meter I became conscious of certain of its features which had not occurred to me before.

This modern gadget treats all cars with impartiality. The shiny Cadillac of this year's vintage gets no more time than does the battered, rusty little Ford which has served for many years. Both are alike to the meter, which says to them, "No more than one hour."

There are some people who take care of their affairs in less than the permitted hour. Can they complain that they have been cheated, that they paid for a full hour and used only a portion of it? The answer obviously is in the negative. The meter never owes you any time, so that you cannot come back another day and have a claim for the time you did not use.

On the other hand, there are those who cannot get their business done within the limits set by the meter. This is regrettable, but nothing can be done about it. One must learn to regulate his affairs according to the time allotted to him. When that period is over, he may not park any longer but must move on, making room for others who will take his space.

Suppose a person desires to outwit the meter and decides to put in several dimes, thus hoping to prolong his parking time. Does it help him in any way? If you are familiar with the workings of the instrument, you realize that no matter how much money you may have, you can only get one hour of time from it. Putting in more money will give you no more privileges.

It is interesting to me that when the hour is up the meter uses the word "expired." Haven't I seen that word used in some other connection? Perhaps we should check its different meanings in the dictionary.

Yes, the parking meter is a fascinating invention to think about when one's mind isn't occupied with more weighty matters. It seems to me that one can learn a great deal from it. And, now that I think about it, it occurs to me that I have never seen a parking meter near a cemetery. Strange, isn't it?

Memory is a divine gift bestowed on man in order to save his life from becoming a meaningless procession of unconnected events. It is the faculty which enables us to make of the past a present reality and to see time as an endless flow of the life process. The sights which we behold, the sounds we hear, the joy we experience—all of these would be merely pictures, projected on life's screen, to be quickly erased, were it not for the power of memory.

Fortunately, we, as human beings, have been given the ability to recall the sun's brilliant rays after it has set, to hear the melody which survives the instrument which has produced it, to feel the glow of a happiness which has departed. It is memory which acts as manna from heaven to nourish the famished spirit, traveling in the wastelands of life.

What is the history of a people but its common memories etched deeply in the mind? The Jews, who were probably the first people on earth with a sense of history, understood the need for preserving memories. In all his festivals, the Jew was reminded of his past. He recognized that the present was a continuation of the past and a preparation for the future. The present tense of the Hebrew verb is as much an adjective as a verb.

It must be admitted, however, that memory does not always bring joy. It may serve to illumine once more some dark corner of the past which it were best to leave in obscurity. Nevertheless, even this is important for a mature person because it teaches us humility in the presence of life, it makes us aware of the price which living demands and of man's precarious situation.

No event of any significance happens to us without leaving some trace behind. We try hard to remember the joys and would like to obliterate the sorrows, but both survive in the mind. For some, the tracings are clear; while with others the impressions are dim. The letters of the Hebrew word meaning "to forget," if rearranged slightly, spell the word meaning "to darken." Forgetfulness means plunging a past experience into darkness, while memory means to see it in a clear light. To be able to say, "I remember," marks one as a human being.

One of the chief sources of unhappiness for a great many people is to be found in regret over the past, in torturing oneself because of what might have been, or what might have been done. A mature person regrets his failure to study in his youth, a woman bemoans the fact that she might have achieved distinction in some career, a child rues his or her lack of consideration for a parent who is deceased, a man is troubled as he contemplates the large amount of money he could have made. In every walk of life and on many age levels we meet people who are miserable because they would like to relive or change the past and find this to be impossible.

If only we would learn that there is no insurance against error, if we would recognize that hindsight is better than foresight, that, in the words of the ancient sages, "What our judgment cannot accomplish, time is able to achieve"—we would be happier human beings. All of life is dependent on choice, and the progress of civilization confronts us with a wider area of choice. This makes life more difficult but also more interesting. The lower animals do not have many decisions to make, and therefore even if they had the capacity to do so, they would have little reason for regret. To make a decision always means to risk the possibility of being sorry afterwards. In this sense all of life is a gamble, and if we do not gamble we are left in a pathetic state of indecision.

We who are grown up, I am sure, remember our childhood when we were given one penny to buy some candy. With joyful anticipation we ran to the local candy store, and there our happiness was dimmed by the variety before us. Carefully did we ponder our choice, and then, after changing our mind several times, we picked what we thought we liked best. Oh, if we only had more money to buy more of these tempting candies! But, alas, all we had was one penny. As we trudged home sucking on or chewing our candy we often felt that we might have made a better choice, but we realized that we could not return the "used merchandise."

We are given only one life and we must use it as seems best to us in those moments when great decisions have to be made. The "candy" we buy is that which we must eat. We don't have a dime or a quarter but only one cent. Perhaps if we'd chosen something else it would have been equally unsatisfying. An old adage admonishes us not to cry over spilt milk, and this is sound advice. In the first place, the milk may have been sour; and, in the second place, it isn't entirely wasted because the water in it may help to dampen the soil and enable it to produce something of value to human beings.

A bright sun shines upon a piece of ground which is full of gravel, sand, and broken slabs of stone on which one can with difficulty discern words. A portion of Jewish history goes through one's mind as he gazes upon these tragic remnants of what must have been an intriguing story of adventure, hope, perhaps success, or maybe, failure.

I stand in the Jewish cemetery on the island of Barbados. It is not very far from the main street of this Caribbean island and is hardly noticed by those who happen to pass it. But it tells a tale of Jewish living and suffering. For here, as to other places in this general area, came Jews who wanted to escape persecution to preserve their traditions, and to maintain their families in an honorable fashion.

One need not have much imagination to write the life story of those whose names are recorded on these tombstones. Many of them died about three hundred years ago, before the American War of Independence, before Washington was born, before there was a Jewish community of any size in the Western Hemisphere. We can hardly appreciate the courage which was demanded for Jews from Holland and Spain to come to this place and gain a foothold in a land peopled by black natives whose way of life was so strange to European Jews.

But as I stood in the Barbados cemetery, I thought of something beyond the Jewish people. I pondered on life and death and immortality.

It is certain that the Jews who lie buried in the broken-down cemetery desired to live on beyond the span of life they were granted here. Leaving aside all theological speculation concerning the nature of life beyond the grave, there can be no doubt that this woman, who died at the age of thirty-seven and upon whose tombstone I gazed, wanted to feel that after death she would not be forgotten. Even if her kin still live here, I doubt whether after two hundred years, she is still remembered by anyone.

Perhaps it would be more assuring and of greater value if we beheld our immortality in our lifetime. Perhaps we need to learn to cherish certain events, certain moments in our lives, as things of which death cannot cheat us. Perhaps immortality can be like a photograph which catches an individual in a mood or an action which remains unchanged over the years. To have tasted the joys of companionship and love, to have listened to the sound of laughter, to have gazed upon some beautiful aspect of nature which God has so plenteously provided around us, and then to expire means that there will go with us that which remains immortal for us. Immortality may perhaps be regarded as a quality of life rather than a hope after death. To have joy and delight in living is more important than to yearn for comfort after death. I wish I were convinced that those who lie in this Caribbean cemetery had found fulfillment in life. If they did, it matters little what is inscribed on their tombstones.

How does one react to an outpouring of loyalty, an expression of respect and a demonstration of love from hundreds of people? An utterance of profound gratitude is the most which is granted to us. But after all that has been said and done, one finds himself in a serious contemplative mood, and in this mood there is a prayer in my heart. It says:

Lord, make me worthy of all the praise and expression of love by the people I have the privilege to serve.

Make me able to show how much I appreciate the kindness which young and old have shown me.

Enable me to comprehend the language of those who cannot put into words the deepest yearnings of their hearts.

Give me the ability and the wisdom to help raise the fallen, to strengthen the weak, to guide the perplexed.

Strengthen my resolve not to use unworthy means to attain even those goals which are most desirable.

Teach me to understand the bitterness and hostility of human beings whose frustrations are visited upon their fellowmen.

Deepen my understanding of Thy word so that I may transmit its eternal significance to those whom I have chosen to teach.

Let me live my life in such a way that I may be able to contribute to the welfare of my fellowmen, and help to restore and maintain peace among those who are created in Thy image.

May I never fail to be grateful for every blessing which has come to me at Thy hand, for the blessings of family and home, the comforts of life and the never-ceasing hope of tomorrow.

Above all, I pray, O Lord, that I may always be humble; that neither honors nor praise may make me haughty; that I may always remember my shortcomings and recognize my limitations, and in all that I do, walk humbly with Thee, O Lord.